alcoholism

Epilepsy, Sleep and Dreams, Life in the Universe, Unusual Partners, Rats and Mice, The Origin of Life, The Respiratory System, A Star in the Sea, A World in a Drop of Water, Cells: Building Blocks of Life, Carl Linnaeus, Frederick Sanger, Germfree Life, Living Lights, Circulatory Systems, The Digestive System, Bionics, Harold Urey, Metamorphosis: The Magic Change, Mammals of the Sea, The Nervous System, The Sense Organs, The Endocrine System, The Reproductive System, The Code of Life, Guinea Pigs, The Long Voyage, The Muscular System, The Skeletal System, Cancer, The Skin, The Excretory System, Exploring the Brain, The Chemicals We Eat and Drink, Rabbits: All About Them, Animal Invaders, Hamsters: All About Them, Oranges, Beans

alcoholism

DR. ALVIN SILVERSTEIN
and VIRGINIA B. SILVERSTEIN

With an Introduction by
Gail Gleason Milgram, Ed.D.,
Consulting Editor

J. B. LIPPINCOTT COMPANY   PHILADELPHIA AND NEW YORK

PRINTED IN THE UNITED STATES OF AMERICA

9

U.S. Library of Congress Cataloging in Publication Data

Silverstein, Alvin.
  Alcoholism.

  Bibliography: p.
  Includes index.
  SUMMARY: Discusses the major aspects of alcohol use and
abuse, including alcohol's chemical composition, its effect on the
body, causes and treatment of alcoholism, teenage drinking, and
living with an alcoholic parent.
  1. Alcoholism—Juvenile literature. 2. Alcohol—Physiological
effect—Juvenile literature. 3. Alcoholism—Treatment—Juvenile
literature. [1. Alcohol. 2. Alcoholism] I. Silverstein, Virginia
B., joint author. II. Title.
HV5066.S54   362.2'92   75-17938
ISBN-0-397-31648-8   ISBN-0-397-31649-6 (pbk.)

Contents

Introduction

Though alcoholic beverages are consumed by the majority of adults and adolescents in the United States, many people have ambivalent feelings about alcohol and its use. Most people know very little about alcohol and its effects, even though they may have a large supply of liquor, serve it often, and may be heavy drinkers. The lack of knowledge about alcohol can be traced through the history of alcohol education. In the early 1900s the "evils" of alcohol were emphasized. By the 1940s alcoholism as a potential threat was the major stress. It wasn't until the 1950s that the main concern of alcohol education was stated to be objective, scientific, and honest information about all aspects of alcohol. Unfortunately the textbooks for young people did not follow the stated goal and most of the materials did not relate to the experiences of adolescents regarding alcohol use. It has only been in recent years that some quality alcohol education materials have been written for young people. *Alcoholism* by Dr. and Mrs. Silverstein is certainly one of the finest.

Alcoholism treats the subject in a way that will be of special interest to teenage readers but will have a wider audience because it is not about teenage problem drinking but about alcoholism in general. Its content covers the major aspects of alcohol use, as well as abuse. In a very informative and pleasurable manner the process of producing alcohol is explained. Types of alcoholic beverages and the alcohol content of the various beverages are clearly described. The text also details the effects of alcohol on the human body and the process by which the body eliminates and oxidizes alcohol. Reasons for alcohol use and nonuse are rationally presented. The disease of alcoholism, a major public health problem, is described and various types of available treatment are presented. The questions asked by most people, alcohol users and nonusers, are covered in the content in an honest, informative, and factual way. The text is also written with a youthful perspective, a statement which can only be made about a very few books today. Teenage drinking is discussed in an objective manner, without the slightest hint of being "preachy." The problems of living with an alcoholic parent are presented in a sympathetic and understanding fashion. As with all of the sections in the text, not only are facts presented but sources of help or additional information are listed.

Alcoholism is not only informative; it is enjoyable reading, providing facts in a manner which sustains interest. It is not a difficult book to read; vocabulary has been chosen to facilitate easy reading. *Alcoholism* was truly written to be read, understood, and enjoyed by anyone who wants to learn the facts about alcohol and alcohol abuse.

Gail Gleason Milgram, Ed.D.
Associate Professor
Center of Alcohol Studies
Rutgers University

The Number One Problem

Alcohol—for many it means a pleasant, relaxing beverage. For some it is a "hard drug," the object of a craving so intense that it may seem to be the only real and important part of life. It is the object of more conflicting, contradictory, and sometimes hypocritical attitudes than perhaps any other aspect of modern life. Some view drinking as a sign of manliness, or think of alcohol as a symbol of being "grown up." A comedian slurs his words and staggers, playing the part of a congenial drunk, and his audience laughs hysterically; meanwhile millions of families struggle with the day-to-day heartbreak of trying to live with an alcoholic. A man buying a bottle of Scotch in a state-licensed liquor store feels vaguely guilty, even though he is performing a perfectly legal act; while at a party, a young woman who has just asked for a "screwdriver without the vodka" feels guilty about *not* drinking. Advocates of abstinence tell horrifying tales of the dangers of drink, while millions of dollars' worth of advertising extols the virtues of various brands of beer, wine, and distilled spirits.

The use and abuse of mind drugs—from marijuana to heroin, amphetamines, barbiturates, LSD and other psychedelics—is one of the major worries of today's public health workers, law enforcement personnel, and the general public. Yet, according to a special Health, Education, and Welfare Department report to the nation in 1971, *alcohol* is the most abused drug in the United States, and the rate of alcoholism is on the rise. According to more recent figures, gathered by the National Institute on Alcohol Abuse and Alcoholism, alcoholism is the nation's third-largest health problem, after heart disease and cancer. It accounts for thirteen thousand deaths each year from cirrhosis of the liver alone, and alcohol is implicated in numerous cases of heart disease, infectious diseases, murders and suicides, industrial accidents, and at least half the deaths and injuries on the highways. The cost of alcoholism to the nation, including lost work time, may come to as much as 15 billion dollars a year.

Yet about 95 million Americans do drink. And for every drinker who is an alcoholic or a problem drinker (one whose drinking hurts himself and society), there are ten or fifteen whose drinking is responsible and controlled. For the majority, alcohol is not a personal problem.

What should be done about alcohol abuse? Certainly a health problem of such magnitude cannot be ignored. Attempts to eliminate the source of the problem, alcoholic beverages, would infringe on the rights of a large fraction of the population who wish to drink and do so appropriately. Moreover, such attempts in the past have generally been dismal failures. A better approach would be to seek more knowledge of the problem: What causes alcoholism? Who runs the greatest risk of becoming an alcoholic? How can problem drinking be treated and cured? It is only recently that alcoholism has begun to be regarded as a disease, rather than a moral failing. Now that research on alcoholism has finally become respectable, the beginnings of answers are emerging.

Meanwhile, to drink or not to drink, and how to drink, is a highly personal decision. It is an especially important question for today's young people. Laws prohibit the sale or serving of alcoholic beverages to minors, yet surveys show that most teenagers do drink. In some ways their drinking helps to prepare them for a role in adult society, in which social drinking is the norm. Yet for various reasons, teenagers and young adults are especially vulnerable to the dangers of alcohol abuse. To make sensible decisions, they need knowledge—not hysterical preachments or the blandishments of advertising, but the "straight story"—the facts about what alcohol is and how it affects the body, the history of drinking and how it has shaped our present attitudes toward drinking, and information about the overhanging problem of alcoholism and its effects on our society.

Alcoholic Beverages

The first alcoholic beverages probably were discovered accidentally, back in the days of the Stone Age. The raw materials are all readily available: sugar in fruits, honey, or sprouted seeds; and microscopic yeast cells, carried in the air. The yeasts get their energy for living and reproducing by acting chemically on sugars, in a reaction called fermentation. In the chemist's "shorthand," the fermentation reaction looks like this:

$$C_6H_{12}O_6 \overset{\text{yeast}}{\rightarrow} 2C_2H_5OH + 2CO_2$$

| glucose | ethyl | carbon |
| (a sugar) | alcohol | dioxide |

When a chemist speaks of "alcohol," he usually is referring to a whole family of chemical compounds that differ in many ways but share one feature in common: their molecules all contain an oxygen atom

(O) and a hydrogen atom (H), linked together to form a combination called a hydroxyl group (OH). The alcohol family includes methyl, or wood, alcohol (CH_3OH); isopropyl, or rubbing, alcohol (C_3H_7OH); and a number of other, more complicated varieties. But the "alcohol" most people refer to when they use the word is ethyl alcohol (C_2H_5OH). This is the alcohol found in fermented beverages. (Though methyl alcohol has occasionally been tried as a substitute drink, it is highly poisonous and may cause blindness or even death.)

The carbon dioxide produced in fermentation, along with the alcohol, is a gas. In baking, yeasts are added to the dough for the carbon dioxide they produce, not for the alcohol; the gas makes the dough rise, and then the heat of baking kills the yeasts before the alcohol content in the bread or cake gets very high. (The alcohol that has been formed evaporates during baking.) In some fermented beverages, the carbon dioxide escapes into the air. Other alcoholic drinks are made in such a way as to keep some carbon dioxide trapped in the liquid, producing a carbonated or "bubbly" drink such as beer or champagne.

Yeast fermentation often occurs in nature. Cows that have been feeding on fallen fruit in an orchard may stagger tipsily. Squirrels and birds may gorge themselves on fermented fruits or berries and then act positively drunk. Though the first alcoholic beverages consumed by humans were undoubtedly just such accidental discoveries, people who liked the effects soon learned how to ferment sugars on purpose and gradually modified and improved on the systems nature provided. People in different parts of the world used different raw materials—whatever was most readily available. Wine was made from grapes and other fruits, and a "wine" called mead was made from honey. In Europe, oats and barley were fermented to make beer and ale. In the Far East, the native grain, rice, yielded fermented beverages such as sake in Japan and tchoo in China. In Central Asia, a fermented drink called koumiss was made from mare's milk.

Many different varieties of alcoholic beverages were produced, depending on the raw materials used and the way the fermentation was conducted. But all the natural fermentation reactions have an important limitation: when the alcohol content reaches about 14 percent, the yeasts can no longer grow and the fermentation stops. No stronger alcoholic beverages could be produced until an entirely new technique was invented: distillation.

Perhaps you have noticed that when water is boiled in a covered pot, steam rises from the boiling liquid, then condenses when it hits the cooler lid and forms liquid drops that eventually drip back into the pot. The heat of the stove raises the temperature of the liquid in the pot to its boiling point; at that time the water evaporates (changes into a gas). But when the water vapor (gas) meets a cooler surface, it transfers part of its heat and changes back into a liquid form. What if the water were heated in a kettle instead—a kettle with a very long spout which led down into a cooled container? As the water vapor condensed, liquid water would accumulate in the container. This is the basic principle of distillation—the heating of a liquid until it turns into a gas, followed by its condensation into a liquid again.

Different substances have different boiling points. Water boils at 212°F (100°C). Ethyl alcohol has a lower boiling point: 173°F (78.5°C). If a mixture of ethyl alcohol and water is heated, the alcohol will distill off at a temperature at which water is still a liquid. Distillation can thus be used to make beverages with a much higher alcohol content than 14 percent. (Under special conditions, 100 percent or "absolute" alcohol can be produced. It is a useful solvent in the laboratory and in industry, but absolute alcohol is not much use as a drink, for it does not contain any of the flavoring agents or other congeners that give alcoholic beverages their special characteristics.)

Beers commonly contain 4 to 6 percent alcohol, table wines 12 percent, and a fortified wine such as sherry may contain 20 percent alcohol. (In a fortified wine, distilled alcohol is added to a wine produced by fermentation to raise its alcohol content.) Distilled beverages such as whiskey usually contain between 40 and 50 percent alcohol by volume.

BEER AND ALE

Beers and ales are made from cereal grains—barley, rye, corn, or wheat. They are made by a process called brewing, which is somewhat more complicated than a simple fermentation. The cereal grains contain starch, not sugar—so the first step in brewing is to change the starch into sugar, on which the yeasts can work. The grains are ground and mixed with water to form a mash. (Other starchy substances such as potatoes can also be used for the mash.) Meanwhile, grains are sprouted in warm water. During sprouting, an enzyme that can change starch to sugar is formed in the seeds. Then the sprouted seeds are heated in an oven (which kills the seed but does not destroy the enzyme) and ground. The product is called the malt, and it is added to the mash. Hops (tiny dried flower buds of the hop vine) are added for flavor, and yeast is added to start the fermentation. After a week or two, the fermentation is stopped. Beer and ale contain various congeners, including dextrins, maltose, vitamins and minerals, organic acids, salts, and carbon dioxide. The congeners give the beverages their characteristic flavors (two thousand varieties of beer are sold in the British Isles alone) and provide some food value. The carbonation is responsible for the foamy "head."

The most common form of beer drunk in the United States today is lager beer, a bright, clear, light-bodied variety originally brewed in Germany. Stout is a dark beer with a sweet taste. Porter is a kind of ale with a heavy foam. The "beere" that the Pilgrims and other early settlers of the United States drank was actually a kind of ale. Generally, ales have a higher alcohol content than beers, and more hops are added during their brewing.

WINES

The appreciation of the varied flavors of wines has been developed to a fine art among wine connoisseurs around the world, and single bottles of a vintage year may command princely sums. Yet at the other end of the scale, Skid Row "winos" are well aware that inexpensive wines offer the largest amount of alcohol for the cheapest price.

The term "wine" originally referred only to fermented grape juice, but it now is commonly used for fermented drinks made from other fruits as well, such as peaches, pears, apricots, and blackberries. (A wine can even be made from flowers such as dandelions.) In making wines, the fermentation is generally allowed to proceed until it stops naturally, at about 14 percent alcohol. Additional alcohol may be added, to produce a fortified wine such as sherry, muscatel, or port. If some unfermented sugar remains in the wine, it has a sweet taste and is referred to as sweet. If no sugar remains, the wine is a dry wine. (In speaking of wines, "dry" is used in this special sense as the opposite of "sweet" and has nothing to do with the amount of water in the beverage.)

Another common classification of wines distinguishes red wines and white wines. Red wines are made from dark grapes, while white wines may be made from white grapes or from black grapes. When black grapes are used, the skins are removed before fermentation begins, so that the coloring does not get into the wine. But no white wines are really colorless —they vary from a pale straw color to a deep amber.

The growing of wine grapes is a complicated art. Not only the variety of grapes but the soil in which they are grown and the weather during the growing season affect the quality and taste of the wine that is made from them. After the grapes are gathered and crushed, they are fermented first in large vats. Gradually the skins, pips, and other solid materials float to the top. The liquid below this layer, called must, is slowly transformed into wine. After a time (from a week to a month), the new wine is drawn off into wooden casks, where the fermentation continues. Solid impurities fall to the bottom of the cask, forming a sediment called lees. The wine is drawn off into a new cask several times, for long contact with the lees might spoil its quality. Finally (after several years for the better wines), the wine is bottled. It continues its fermentation for a time in the glass bottles.

Sparkling wines, such as champagne or sparkling Burgundy, are wines that contain carbon dioxide. The gas may be produced naturally by fermentation, or it may be pumped into the wine after fementation has ceased.

DISTILLED SPIRITS

Ancient peoples, who observed the strange effects of drinking fermented juices, thought that supernatural spirits in the wine were responsible. During the Middle Ages, when Europeans learned how to distill alcohol from wine, they referred to it as "spirits of wine." Today the supernatural connotations are gone, but we still commonly refer to alcoholic beverages as spirits.

The fluid that distills off from fermented grains or fruits contains a high content of alcohol, together with water and various small amounts of flavoring ingredients (congeners). The raw spirits are diluted with water to the proper concentration for drinking and may be aged in charred wooden barrels, which adds to the unique flavors.

The alcohol content of distilled beverages is commonly expressed in a scale called "proof," which is exactly twice the percentage of alcohol by volume. Thus, a 100 proof whiskey contains 50 percent alcohol. (The term "Bottled in Bond," which is sometimes found on the labels of whiskeys such as rye and bourbon, refers to a whiskey that has been bottled at 100 proof and stored for at least four years in a bonded warehouse.) Whiskeys are often 86 proof (i.e., contain 43 percent alcohol); gins vary from 80 to 94 proof, and rum and brandy are commonly 80 proof.

Whiskey is made from cereal grains, such as corn, rye, and barley. Bourbon, made mainly from fermented corn, and rye, made from rye, are classified as straight whiskeys. (Actually, a mixture of grains may be fermented; the whiskey is named for the grain that predominates in the mixture.) In blended whiskeys, neutral spirits (almost pure ethyl alcohol, 190 proof or more) are mixed with straight whiskeys in careful proportions.

Scotch whisky (spelled without the *e* both in Scotland and in Canada) is made in Scotland from barley or corn. It has a distinctive smoky flavor that comes from drying the sprouted barley malt over peat fires.

Gin is a combination of neutral spirits and various flavoring agents such as juniper berries, orange or lemon peel, cassia bark, and anise. Each distiller prepares his product according to a formula that is a carefully guarded secret.

Vodka is a mixture of practically pure ethyl

alcohol and water, and it is close to colorless, odorless, and tasteless. In its native Russia, vodka is distilled mainly from potatoes, while in the United States it is usually produced from fermented grain mash.

Rum is a distilled spirit produced from fermented sugarcane juice or molasses. The most famous rums are made in the West Indies.

Brandies are distilled from wine or from fermented fruit mashes. Cognac is a brandy distilled from grapes and takes its name from a region of France. Slivovitz is a plum brandy that is the national beverage of Hungary, Rumania, and Yugoslavia. Kirsch is a colorless brandy produced from black cherries that grow in the Rhine basin. Most brandies are sweet drinks; they are sometimes used in cooking or combined with coffee.

Liqueurs are very sweet distilled beverages which contain flavorings such as fruits, juices, herbs, or flowers, along with at least 2½ percent sugar. They are usually sipped slowly in small amounts.

Some people drink distilled spirits "straight" (unmixed with other beverages) or "on the rocks" (poured over ice). Others prefer highballs or mixed drinks. A highball consists of whiskey or another liquor, diluted with water or a carbonated beverage, and served in a tall glass with ice. A cocktail is a mixture of a distilled spirit with various combinations of wine, water, carbonated beverages, fruit juices, or other flavorings. Manhattans and martinis are commonly served cocktails containing about three parts distilled spirits to one part vermouth, a wine flavored with wormwood and other herbs.

Alcoholic beverages vary greatly in their alcoholic content. Beer, for example, contains about twenty parts of nonalcoholic fluid to one part of ethyl alcohol, while sherry wine is about 20 percent alcohol, a cocktail may be 40 percent alcohol, and a straight whiskey 50 percent alcohol. The sizes of typical servings of alcoholic beverages also vary, however, and a twelve-ounce can of beer, five ounces of table wine, and an ounce and a half of a cocktail or whiskey all contain roughly the same amount of alcohol—between half and three-quarters of an ounce. The effects of this alcohol on the body may be quite different, though, depending on the kind of beverage. Generally, the higher the dilution of the alcohol with water or other nonalcoholic substance, the smaller the effect. Very concentrated alcoholic beverages, on the other hand, tend to irritate the lining of the stomach and intestines and slow down the rate of absorption of alcohol into the bloodstream. So a person may get drunk faster on a wine or highball. The rate of drinking, the nonalcoholic ingredients in drinks, food eaten before or during drinking, the drinker's experience and physical condition, and the social setting in which the drinks are consumed are other important factors influencing the effects of alcohol, as we shall see in later chapters.

What Alcohol Does in the Body

A generation or two ago, typical lectures in high school classes on the dangers of alcohol began with a dramatic demonstration. The speaker dropped an earthworm into a clear glass containing alcohol. Within minutes, the worm shriveled up and died. "That is just what alcohol does to a person's liver and brain," the speaker would declare, going on to expand upon the perils of drinking.

Such dramatic demonstrations really prove very little, other than that earthworms should avoid bathing in concentrated alcohol. (Indeed, being dropped into a glass of pure water would be equally fatal for the worm.) Exhibits in which an egg was broken into a glass of whiskey, and the white coagulated as though it were being "cooked," were not very convincing either to anyone with some knowledge of what actually happens to beverage alcohol in the body.

The 40 to 50 percent concentrations of alcohol

present in distilled spirits can indeed be irritating to the delicate mucous membranes lining the mouth and throat. The husky "whiskey voice" that some heavy drinkers develop is evidence of such damage. But before any alcohol can reach the liver or brain, it must first pass into the bloodstream, where it is greatly diluted in the body fluids. A single highball or cocktail or two bottles of beer will raise the alcohol concentration in the blood to only about 0.03 percent. In most states, a driver stopped on the highway by the police is considered to be "under the influence" if his blood alcohol level is above 0.1 percent. Such an alcohol solution is so dilute that it could be used as a mild eyewash without any irritation. Even prolonged heavy drinking could not raise the alcohol level in the blood and body fluids high enough to cause brain and liver tissues to shrivel or "cook"; but blood alcohol levels much above half a percent can result in coma and even death. Alcohol does have profound effects on the body, which may be harmful and dangerous. But they are far more subtle and complicated than the oversimplified demonstrations with worms and eggs would imply.

Like other foods and drinks, alcoholic beverages are normally swallowed and pass down the esophagus into the stomach. Most food materials are rather complicated chemicals. A typical protein molecule, for example, contains thousands of atoms. Before most foods can be absorbed into the bloodstream and distributed through the body, they must first be broken down into smaller fragments in the process of digestion. But the ethyl alcohol molecule, C_2H_5OH, is already a rather small molecule, even smaller than most simple sugars, amino acids, and other end products of digestion. Ethyl alcohol therefore does not need to be digested before it is absorbed into the body.

For most foods, the stomach acts as a sort of mill, in which solids are churned by muscle action while hydrochloric acid and enzymes break down the large molecules into smaller fragments. Little by little, the partly digested food materials are squirted through a circular opening at the bottom of the stomach, called the pylorus, into the small intestine. There further digestion occurs, and only then are the food materials absorbed into the bloodstream through the lining of the intestine.

The absorption of alcohol does not follow this usual pattern. About one-fifth of the alcohol taken into the stomach is absorbed directly through the walls of the stomach. The remaining 80 percent is absorbed through the walls of the intestines, a process that is much more rapid than the absorption from the stomach.

The rate of absorption of alcohol into the bloodstream is an important factor determining how fast a drink "goes to your head." In turn, it is determined by many things. One of these is the degree of dilution of the original drink. Beer, containing perhaps 20 parts of water to one part alcohol, does not raise the blood alcohol level as rapidly as drinks of wine or liquor containing the same total amount of alcohol in more concentrated form. (The small amounts of food substances in beer also tend to slow absorption.) But in many people, highly concentrated alcoholic drinks, such as a straight whiskey, irritate the stomach, particularly the pylorus. The ringlike muscle at the bottom of the stomach tightens and prevents the stomach contents from passing into the intestines, where more alcohol would be absorbed, more rapidly. If the irritation is severe enough, the drinker may vomit, eliminating the alcohol from his or her body completely. Carbonation of alcoholic beverages speeds up the absorption of alcohol by relaxing the pyloric valve, permitting more alcohol to pass from the stomach into the intestines—champagne really does go to your head faster than other wines of the same alcohol concentration that are not so bubbly.

Food in the stomach also dilutes the alcohol in drinks, slowing down its absorption. Experienced drinkers who want to be able to "hold their liquor" at a party may coat their stomachs beforehand by drinking milk or eating eggs. Foods rich in fats or proteins seem especially effective in moderating the effects of alcohol. A person who is drinking specifically "to get high" may prefer to speed up the effects of alcohol by drinking on an empty stomach.

The size of a person's body is another important factor in how well he or she can "hold liquor." If a two-hundred-pound person and a one-hundred-pound person both drink the same amount of alcohol in the same amount of time, the lighter person will show more effect, more quickly. It has been calculated that a person's body tissues are about 70 percent water. So a heavier person has much more body water in which alcohol can be diluted. An exception is a very fat person, whose extra weight is mainly fatty tissue, which contains relatively little water. So a drink will produce a higher alcohol level in the fat person's blood and tissues, as though he or she actually weighed much less.

The amount of alcohol in a drink is an obvious factor influencing its effects on the body. A bottle of beer, a glass of wine, and a shot of whiskey all contain roughly the same amount of alcohol, even though their total volumes are quite different. The rate of consumption is another important factor. The more slowly a person drinks, the more slowly alcohol is absorbed into the body. The volume and dilution of a drink has another, subtle effect here: it is much easier to sip a highball and make it last; a cocktail containing the same amount of alcohol in a much smaller volume tends to be finished more quickly.

Curiously, the amount of experience a drinker has had with alcoholic beverages also influences the apparent effects of alcohol. An inexperienced drinker may quickly become intoxicated after a drink or two, while an experienced drinker may down the same amount with very little visible change. Part of the cause may lie in a greater ability of the experienced drinker's body to handle and dispose of alcohol. Great individual variations in the ability of the body to eliminate alcohol have been found, and a habitual drinker can build up a considerable tolerance to alcohol. (Yet after years of heavy drinking, this alcohol tolerance may suddenly be lost, and a heavy drinker get intoxicated on much smaller amounts of alcohol than before.) In addition, an experienced drinker has usually learned to compensate for the effects of alcohol, so that little outward change may be noticed.

Just what are the effects of alcohol on the body, after it is absorbed into the bloodstream?

The first effect of alcohol that is noticed by the drinker is a feeling of relaxation and warmth. It is popularly believed that alcohol is a stimulant. After a drink or two, a person may become gay, talkative, laughing easily and often. The "life of the party," clowning around with a lampshade on his head, is a typical picture that comes to mind. Yet alcohol is not really a stimulant at all. It belongs to a group of drugs classed as depressants. It has an inhibiting effect on the central nervous system (the brain and spinal cord), slowing down and damping the action of the nerves. The reason that alcohol seems to have a stimulant effect at first is that it inhibits some of the controls the conscious brain normally exerts on a person's actions. Instead of constantly thinking first about the consequences of what they are going to say or do, drinkers tend to express whatever thoughts come to their minds, and do things that they might not do while sober. The feeling of warmth is caused by another effect of alcohol on the body: it produces a widening or dilation of the blood vessels in the skin, increasing the flow of blood to the surface of the body. Despite the feeling of warmth, the drinker's body is actually being cooled at a rapid rate, for the blood flow to the heart and other internal organs is reduced, and body heat is radiated out from the drinker's flushed skin.

After two or three drinks, the drinker's coordination begins to be affected, and the ability to concentrate and think clearly may be impaired. The drinker may have trouble balancing and walking straight and may begin to slur words when talking. He may think that his mind is very sharp and creative. Indeed, some tests of people's ability to associate words and solve problems in logic after drinking a moderate amount of alcohol have shown that they can do as well or better than before drinking. But in other mental tasks their abilities are far below par. A typist, after a few drinks, may be able to type just as rapidly as usual but will make more mistakes than while sober. A driver may feel in perfect control, but may not notice stop signs or pedestrians crossing—and when the driver does notice them, his reactions are slowed. Apparently, different parts of the brain are affected by alcohol at different rates. Many researchers feel that the higher centers, in the cerebral cortex, are affected first. But some others believe that alcohol works first on the reticular formation, deeper in the brain, which acts as a sort of master switchboard in the brain, filtering incoming information and directing the attention of the appropriate centers in the higher brain.

As inhibitions are lost, and the higher centers of the brain cease to exert their normal controls, the drinker's behavior may become more emotional. Drinkers may become elated or depressed. Worries and fears may cease to bother them, and they are able to ignore physical pain. But they may become aggressive, in words or in physical actions. Riots and brawls are far more likely to occur when people have been drinking than when they are sober, and when civil disturbances break out, one of the first things the authorities usually do is to close bars and liquor stores. (Rioters, on the other hand, often choose liquor stores as prime targets for looting.)

Is alcohol an aphrodisiac? Many people find that a few drinks relax them, remove inhibitions, and help to put them in the mood for sex. But as Shakespeare put it, drink "provokes the desire, but takes away the performance." After a number of drinks, a man may find he is unable to complete the actual sex act, even though he wants to.

One effect that drinkers commonly experience is a need to urinate frequently, together with a feeling of thirst. It was thought at one time that this effect was the result of irritation of the lining of the urinary tract and of the extra water the drinker takes in. But it has been found that the effect is more complicated. The elimination of water and other substances by the kidneys, through the production of urine, is regulated by a hormone called antidiuretic hormone (ADH), produced in the pituitary gland. If the body fluids become too concentrated, ADH is secreted and causes the kidneys to return more water to the blood. As a result, a smaller volume of more concentrated urine is produced. But alcohol interferes with the secretion of ADH. Without the hormone, the kidneys produce large volumes of dilute urine. The body fluids grow more and more concentrated as water is lost from the body, and monitoring stations in the brain flash their signals: "Thirsty! Drink more water!"

After additional drinks within a relatively short time, the impairments of mental and physical abilities increase. The drinker has difficulty walking and talking. At a blood alcohol level of 0.2 percent, he or she may be unable to stand up. Feelings of euphoria give way to dazedness and confusion. Drowsiness grows, and by 0.4 percent alcohol in the blood the drinker will become unconscious—pass out. Deep coma sets in at 0.5 percent alcohol, and at 0.6 percent death may result from suppression of the nerve centers that control the heartbeat and breathing. Fortunately, people usually lose consciousness before they are able to literally drink themselves to death, but there have been cases when death resulted from extreme over-drinking in drinking contests.

Some of the effects of alcohol on the body may seem pleasant to the drinker. But, especially when it is taken in excess, alcohol is clearly a poison for the body. We recognize this in calling drunkenness "intoxication"—a "toxin" is a poison. The body does have defenses against alcohol poisoning. From the time that alcohol first enters the bloodstream, the body's systems of elimination begin to work on getting rid of the poison. Perhaps 10 percent of the alcohol taken into the body is eliminated through the lungs, sweat glands, and kidneys. It passes through these excretory organs mostly unchanged: the "alcohol odor" on the breath of someone who has been drinking is exactly that—molecules of ethyl alcohol that have passed from blood capillaries in the lungs into the numerous tiny air sacs and evaporated into the exhaled air. But the other 90 percent of the alcohol goes through a series of chemical reactions in the liver, where it is gradually "detoxified."

The liver is an amazing and much underrated organ. It is like a chemical factory, conducting hundreds of different chemical reactions. In addition to producing bile, which helps in the digestion of fats, and storing reserve sugar in the form of glycogen, the liver is the body's main center for converting poisons to less harmful substances. The liver has an especially rich blood supply. Blood is pumped by the heart around the body through a closed circuit of blood vessels, and it passes through the liver again and again. In the liver, substances in the blood are subjected to the action of numerous enzymes. Alcohol passes through a series of reactions. First it is combined with oxygen, forming a substance called acetaldehyde (CH_3CHO) and water and generating heat. Acetaldehyde is even more toxic to the body than ethyl alcohol. But it is quickly further oxidized (combined with oxygen), both in the liver and in other tissues of the body. In this reaction, acetic acid (CH_3COOH) is formed, and more heat is released. Finally, acetic acid is oxidized further, to carbon dioxide (CO_2) and water, in a reaction that also yields heat. Altogether, a gram of alcohol yields about 7 Calories of heat. In comparison, a gram of sugar or other carbohydrates yields 4 Calories, and a gram of fat yields 9 Calories. Heavy drinking can thus add rather substantially to a person's calorie intake and may lead to a gain of weight. Or the drinker may tend to substitute alcohol calories for food calories, and eat less. But the calories provided by alcohol lack food value. They provide energy, but they cannot be stored for future use, and alcohol cannot be used to build body tissues, as carbohydrates, fats, and proteins can. As a result, heavy drinkers often suffer from nutritional deficiency diseases, in addition to the damaging effects of the alcohol itself.

The reactions by which the body gets rid of alcohol take time. On the average, it has been found that a 150-pound person's body can eliminate about one-third of an ounce of alcohol in an hour. For a typical distilled spirit, that would be equivalent to about three-quarters of an ounce, or half a standard ounce-and-a-half "jigger." In other words, it will take the body about two hours to get rid of the alcohol in one drink, four hours for two drinks, and so on. People who drink at parties and worry about how to get home safely afterward—especially when public transportation is not available, and someone must drive—are understandably concerned about ways to "sober up" faster. Unfortunately, the standard remedies—walking drunken people around, exposing them to "fresh air," and plying them with black coffee—do not speed up the elimination of alcohol, although they may make drinkers alert enough to compensate a little better for the effects of alcohol on their bodies.

Studies on animals at the Veterans Administration Hospital in Tucson, Arizona, have pointed the way to one approach to speeding the sobering up process. The research team, headed by Dr. Cleamond Eskelson, gave rats large doses of vitamins and fructose, a sugar found in fruits and honey, after the rats had consumed alcohol. The blood alcohol levels of the treated rats fell more rapidly than those of untreated rats. A similar approach was later tried on humans by a team of emergency-room physicians in Lynn, Massachusetts. These doctors report that intravenous injections of fructose sober up drunks in two and a half hours or less. But this medical technique is still far from a "sobering pill" that a partygoer could pop before leaving for home. In another approach that may prove promising, rats were given the chemical sodium acetate at the same time as a dose of alcohol. (Sodium acetate is a salt form of one of the products, acetic acid, that is formed in the body's oxidation of alcohol.) It was found that sodium acetate prevented the rats' blood alcohol levels from rising to the level of intoxication, even though the rats were given enough alcohol to keep them drunk for two or three hours under normal conditions.

Once the alcohol is eliminated from a drinker's body, his problems still are not over. Now he may suffer a hangover, a miserable combination of headache, nausea, sensitivity to noise, and general aches and pains. If the drinking bout has been long and heavy, extending over a period of days, weeks, or even months, the effects of withdrawal from alcohol may be far more severe, including hallucinations, severe muscle tremors, and even convulsions. This type of severe withdrawal reaction is referred to as delirium tremens, or D.T.'s. Delirium tremens is not something to take casually; it is a medical emergency, requiring skilled help, and even under a doctor's care it may be fatal.

Some researchers believe that a lack of magnesium is a key factor in the symptoms of withdrawal from alcohol. This element plays an important role in the work of the central nervous system. Under the influence of alcohol, it is excreted by the kidneys in a larger proportion than other metal ions, and its amount in the body falls far more than that of sodium or potassium. Withdrawal symptoms subside when the magnesium is restored.

Studies both on animals and on humans have suggested another intriguing theory explaining alcohol withdrawal symptoms, from hangover to D.T.'s. It has been found that small amounts of alcohols are produced in the normal body—both ethyl alcohol and methyl alcohol. These alcohols are routinely detoxified in the liver, through a series of oxidation reactions successively producing an aldehyde, an acid, and ultimately carbon dioxide. But the formaldehyde formed in the oxidation of methyl alcohol is even more toxic than the acetaldehyde produced from ethyl alcohol. The liver enzymes that handle the oxidation have a pronounced preference for ethyl alcohol, breaking it down sixteen times as rapidly as methyl alcohol. Normally this does not make much difference, for the liver has ample capacity to handle the alcohols that the body produces. But a person who drinks ethyl alcohol floods his liver with it. In the hours that the liver is occupied with detoxifying the ethyl alcohol that the person has drunk, a considerable amount of methyl alcohol builds up, waiting its turn at the enzymes. When the ethyl alcohol has finally been disposed of and the liver enzymes begin to work on the methyl alcohol, considerable formaldehyde is produced and may be responsible for the withdrawal symptoms. In experiments at the National Institute on Alcohol Abuse and Alcoholism, volunteers drank a quart of bourbon or grain alcohol each day for periods of up to two weeks. Measurements of the levels of ethyl and methyl alcohols in their blood during and after these periods showed that the hangover began precisely when the ethyl alcohol levels fell, freeing the enzymes to work on the methyl alcohol that had accumulated.

The effects of alcohol on the body may be greatly influenced by various other drugs, taken before or with the alcohol. Today, when a great variety of drugs are taken by many people for numerous reasons, either occasionally or regularly, such combined effects with alcohol may be especially important.

With antihistamines, commonly taken for colds and allergies, alcoholic beverages can make a person extremely drowsy. Alcohol has a similar effect when drunk by someone who is taking tranquilizers. In each case, there is what scientists refer to as a synergistic effect—two drugs together have an effect that is greater than what would be expected if their individual effects were merely added to each other.

The combination of alcohol with barbiturates is especially dangerous. Barbiturates are sometimes prescribed as sleeping pills. Like alcohol, these drugs are powerful depressants. Alcohol and barbiturates can depress the central nervous system to such an extent that breathing stops and the person dies. Janis Joplin, the rock singer, was one of a number of well-known people who died after taking combinations of alcohol and barbiturates in amounts that separately would only have caused sedation.

Stimulants such as caffeine are often used in an attempt to sober up a drunk. But although caffeine can wake up a sleepy drunk, it does not make the drunk sober—the impairment of coordination and other effects of alcohol will remain until the alcohol is out of the drinker's system. The more powerful stimulants, amphetamines, make an unpredictable and risky mixture with alcohol, similar in effect to a mixture of amphetamines ("uppers") with barbiturates ("downers").

Researchers at Rutgers University have studied the effects of alcohol in combination with another commonly used drug, nicotine. These studies have great practical importance, for most heavy drinkers are also smokers. (In fact, when a group of researchers reported that while smokers have a higher risk of developing cancer of the mouth and throat than nonsmokers, smokers who also drink heavily are even likelier to develop such cancers, their results were criticized. It was pointed out that their study lacked data for a group of heavy drinkers who were nonsmokers. There was a good reason for the omission: researchers have been unable to find enough nonsmoking heavy drinkers to make a statistically valid sample!)

The Rutgers researchers, headed by Henry Murphree, worked with a group of sixteen volunteers, who were given enough vodka and orange juice to raise their blood alcohol level to 0.07 percent. The volunteers were given two types of tests: to duplicate geometric figures fifteen seconds after seeing them, and to keep a pointer on a spot on a slowly moving turntable for two minutes. During the tests, the volunteers either did not smoke, smoked low-nicotine cigarettes, or smoked high-nicotine cigarettes. Later they switched from nonsmoking to smoking, or vice versa. Dr. Murphree expected that nicotine would help the drinkers to concentrate and improve their coordination. But instead, the drinkers who smoked high-nicotine cigarettes did much worse on the tests than those who did not smoke, or smoked low-nicotine cigarettes. Changing from smoking to nonsmoking improved the test results, while changing from non-smoking to high-nicotine cigarettes made the volunteers do worse on the tests.

The main danger in a single drinking episode is the possibility of becoming drunk, with increased chances of having an accident or becoming involved in an act of violence. There have been no reliable studies which indicate that moderate drinking—drinking occasionally, or a regular practice of drinking small amounts of alcohol, perhaps a drink or two each night—causes any long-term harmful effects to the body. Indeed, statistical studies indicate that moderate drinkers live just as long as nondrinkers. But when alcohol is abused, either by going on periodic drinking sprees or by steadily drinking large amounts of alcohol, serious damage to the body may result.

As might be expected, one of the primary sites of damage by alcohol is the liver. According to Dr. Peter Stokes of Cornell University Medical College, after just a few weeks of drinking three or four typical drinks a night, a person's liver becomes fatty and loses some of its efficiency. Fortunately, the liver is one of the few organs of the body that is capable of completely rebuilding itself, if it is given the chance. In the early stages, liver damage can be completely reversed if the drinker abstains. But if heavy alcohol consumption continues, the fatty deposits grow.

After years of alcohol abuse—drinking perhaps a pint or more of whiskey or the equivalent every day—a person's liver cells may be replaced by fibrous scar tissue, damage that cannot be repaired. A smaller and smaller fraction of the liver is able to carry on its normal functions (including the detoxification of alcohol). This condition is called cirrhosis of the liver, and it causes the death of about thirteen thousand Americans each year.

Prolonged abuse of alcohol damages other systems of the body as well. The heart muscle, like the liver, becomes fatty and flabby, and can no longer work efficiently to pump blood through the body. Alcohol abuse thus contributes to many cases of heart disease, the leading cause of death in the United States.

Ironically, many heart patients take a drink each night to relax them and ease the pain of angina (a heart condition in which there are spasms in the chest, with a feeling of suffocation).

A heavy drinker often develops gastritis, an irritation of the lining of the stomach and small intestine which causes stomach pains. Heavy alcohol intake may result in poor eating habits, producing nutritional deficiencies. These conditions often cannot be prevented by taking vitamin pills, for alcohol interferes with the body's ability to use certain vitamins. Alcohol abuse also depresses the production and activity of disease-fighting white blood cells, giving an alcoholic low resistance to bacterial infections.

Studies of children born to alcoholic mothers have shown that alcohol passes through the placenta and can interfere with the baby's development. Such children may be abnormally small at birth and frequently have defects of the joints and heart. The children of malnourished mothers who do not drink alcohol are also small but quickly catch up if they are well fed after birth. The children of alcoholic mothers, however, continue to lag behind normal children.

Perhaps the most frightening changes that prolonged heavy drinking produces in the body are those in the brain. Studies by Drs. Sujata Tewari and Ernest

Noble of the University of California at Irvine have shown that alcohol interferes with the manufacture of RNA and protein in the brains of mice. In both mice and humans, RNA and protein synthesis in the brain plays a key role in learning and the formation and storage of memories. Perhaps this effect of alcohol on the brain's memory-forming mechanisms is the cause of alcoholic "blackouts," in which some drinkers are unable to remember what happened during a period when they were intoxicated. Many studies of the brains of people who died after years of heavy drinking have revealed widespread destruction of brain cells. Since the body cannot produce new brain cells to replace those that have been lost, such damage is irreversible.

Alcohol in History

According to an old Persian myth, alcoholic beverages were discovered by accident. King Jamshid was very fond of grapes. Grapes were stored in jars, so that the king would have a supply of grapes to eat whenever he wished. But one day, when the king pulled out some grapes from a jar, he found that the fruits were no longer sweet. Convinced that the grapes had spoiled and might be dangerous, the king ordered that the jar be labeled "poison."

By coincidence, at that time one of the ladies in King Jamshid's harem was suffering from headaches. The pain was so severe that she decided to kill herself, rather than go on suffering any longer. Finding the jar of "poison" grapes, she drank deeply of their juice. Of course, the grapes were not really poison, but were merely fermented into wine. The suffering concubine was delighted to find that the fermented grape juice not only did not kill her, but relieved her pain. She continued to sip from the jar in secret whenever her headaches bothered her. Finally she was discovered in her solitary drinking, the king was informed, and he had new jars of wine prepared for all the members of the court to share.

The real discovery of fermented beverages probably preceded King Jamshid's time by a couple of million years. But it was undoubtedly just as accidental. Various groups of prehistoric men probably independently discovered the intoxicating effects of fermented fruits and grains and, liking them, learned the secret of making alcoholic drinks for themselves. Archaeologists have found many evidences of alcohol drinking among early peoples. Beer jugs dating back to the late Stone Age have been unearthed. Pottery from Mesopotamia, dating back to about 4200 B.C., shows scenes of fermentation. The ancient Egyptians drank beer, while a favorite god in ancient Greece was Bacchus, the god of wine, whose worship was celebrated with drunken revelry. The early Romans disapproved of drunkenness, but drinking wine to excess became very fashionable in the times of the Roman emperors.

The Bible contains numerous references to wine, which "maketh glad the heart of man." Noah, the righteous man saved from the Flood, planted a vineyard, made wine from his grapes, and "became drunken." Samson, Daniel, Solomon, Jeremiah, and John the Baptist all spoke of the use of wine.

The earliest references to alcohol in India date back to about 2000 B.C. In China, drinks made from fermented rice and millet were known in ancient times, and distillation was invented around 800 B.C.

The religion founded in the Near East by Mohammed emphasized abstinence from alcoholic beverages of all kinds. This teaching was a reaction to the widespread drunkenness and alcohol abuse that prevailed in Mohammed's time, and it brought a revolution in the attitudes of his followers. Yet ironically it was Mohammedan Arabs who introduced the technique of distillation into Europe around the twelfth century. (The natives were already familiar with various types of fermented beverages.) Our present word *alcohol* comes from the Arabic word *al-kuhul*, or *al-kohl*, which refers to powdered antimony (a black substance used, among other things, as an early form of eye shadow and mascara).

In the Americas, the Aztecs used wine in their religious ceremonies and spread its use among the peoples they conquered. Chicha, a corn beer, was also widely used, but drunkenness was forbidden and punishable by death. Potent distilled beverages were introduced by Spanish conquerors and eventually became a means of subjugating the poor, keeping them content with their lot by providing a means of temporary escape from reality.

Most of the Indians of North America were among the few peoples of the world who had no native traditions of drinking alcoholic beverages. These were introduced by the white settlers.

The Pilgrims and Puritans and other English settlers used beer as a common beverage; Dutch settlers favored their native drink, gin. Rum from the West Indies became so popular in Colonial America that the Revolutionary army received part of its rations in rum. At the time, alcoholic beverages were considered good for the health (in moderation) and necessary to help keep a soldier's strength up.

Some of the Indians introduced to "firewater" by the settlers sipped it cautiously, but others drank to excess. The lack of traditions and social attitudes dealing with drinking left the Indian communities without any normal social controls in this area. Outbreaks of violence sparked by the aggressiveness stimulated by alcohol led to regulations prohibiting the sale of "firewater" to Indians. Such restrictions did not completely eliminate drinking among Indians, but instead encouraged surreptitious drinking. The destructive drinking patterns that developed are still a problem on Indian reservations today.

In the early Colonial days, beer and wine were the usual alcoholic beverages, and they were drunk mainly in the home, in a controlled way. But gradually distilled spirits became more popular in America, and they were often consumed in saloons. Drunkenness and violence due to drinking became common. Together with the growing abuse of alcohol, there was a growing feeling that something ought to be done to control the problem.

The temperance movement that developed in the United States, gaining strength in the second half of the nineteenth century, was really nothing new. Warnings against drunkenness and attempts to control alcohol abuse probably have a history nearly as ancient as the use of alcoholic beverages itself. Egyptian inscriptions from 1500 B.C. caution against excessive drinking of beer. In Athens, although drinking was popular, regulations provided for wine inspectors, the dilution of wine with water, and specified fines for various types of misbehavior "under the influence." Plato recommended even more stringent regulations— restricting the number of vineyards under cultivation, prohibiting praise of drinking, and requiring abstinence by people under eighteen, pregnant women, boat pilots, and slaves. The ancient Chinese had numerous laws regulating the manufacture, distribution, and use of alcohol.

In the United States, as in various other countries at the time, the temperance movement was at first aimed at promoting "temperance" in the original meaning of the word, that is, moderation. Efforts were made to persuade drinkers of the desirability of drinking in moderation, and to promote a shift from "hard liquor" to less intoxicating fermented beverages. But the lack of success of such "moral suasion" gradually led to a shift of emphasis, from moderation to total abstinence. Alcoholic beverages were attacked as being not only unnecessary, but harmful to health and poisonous. Temperance boosters became convinced that anyone who took a drink of hard liquor was immediately doomed to become a habitual drunkard.

Women were at the forefront of the American temperance movement. They were active in such organizations as the Anti-Saloon League and the Women's Christian Temperance Union. Their efforts at persuasion ranged from songs like "Lips That Touch Liquor Shall Never Touch Mine" and programs of antialcohol education for children to more violent measures. In Kansas, a heroine of the Temperance movement, Carry Nation, left a trail of destruction through the saloons of her state, smashing them with a hatchet.

The efforts of the antialcohol forces were strengthened by a best-selling novel written by Timothy Shay Arthur, *Ten Nights in a Bar Room*. It became a smash hit not only in book form but also in a stage version that played in long runs in theaters throughout the nation. This melodramatic story summed up all the direst predictions of the temperance advocates. Little Mary appeared each night at Sam Slade's tavern to try to persuade her father to come home. (In stage versions, she sang the touching song, "Father, Dear Father, Come Home with Me Now.") Mary was accidentally killed in a drunken brawl in the tavern, and at her deathbed her father promised never to touch a drop of liquor again. Meanwhile, tragedies occurred to other townspeople who continued to go to the tavern to drink. A promising young man was killed by a gambler; a prominent judge went to the poorhouse, and his wife died insane. Finally, Little Mary's father, the reformed drunkard, led a movement in the community for the passage of laws to abolish drinking. The impact of the book and play in stimulating support for the temperance movement has been compared with the role of *Uncle Tom's Cabin* in sparking the drive for the abolition of slavery.

As the temperance advocates gained strength, various states and localities passed regulations prohibiting the sale and use of alcoholic beverages. But these laws usually proved impossible to enforce and were repealed after a short time. Bitter debates raged between the "wets" and the "drys." The Anti-Saloon League became a powerful political force, and their lobbying helped to push through the Eighteenth Amendment in 1917. Together with the Volstead Act, which set up the machinery for enforcing it, this amendment provided for a complete prohibition of the manufacture, sale, and transportation of intoxicating beverages. By 1919, three-quarters of the states had ratified the Eighteenth Amendment, and Prohibition was the law of the land. The Noble Experiment had begun.

Many theories have been offered to explain why Prohibition did not work. The underlying cause seems to have been the basic fact that when a law is passed that goes against the common practices and beliefs of the majority of the people, the law will be frequently broken, and its existence may promote a disrespect for laws and authority in general. In spite of the laws, "bathtub gin" and other forms of alcohol flowed freely during the "Roaring Twenties." Alcohol was illegally diverted from industrial production to make beverages, and alcoholic drinks were smuggled in from other countries. "Moonshine" trickled out from the mountains of Kentucky and neighboring states, despite the efforts of ax-swinging government agents to put the illegal stills out of business. Because alcoholic beverages were illegal, their distribution came to be associated with organized crime, as heroin and other illegal narcotic drugs are today.

Finally, in 1932, it was acknowledged that the Noble Experiment had failed, and another amendment was passed, repealing Prohibition. Alcoholic beverages are no longer illegal throughout the nation (although there are still a number of local "dry" areas), but the residues of the bitter debate still linger on to influence our attitudes toward drinking and drinking practices today.

Drinking Today--
Social Drinking
and Problem Drinking

About two-thirds of the adults in the United States drink alcoholic beverages. People drink various kinds of alcoholic beverages, in varying amounts, in various ways, and for various reasons.

Beer is the most popular of all the alcoholic beverages in the United States today, accounting for nearly half of all the alcohol consumed. Distilled spirits are not far behind, accounting for somewhat more than 40 percent of the total, and their use seems to be on the rise. Wines currently account for around 10 percent of the total, though the introduction of "pop wines" has sparked a gain in popularity, especially among young people.

Both social drinkers and problem drinkers are found at all social and economic levels, from the poor to the affluent, in cities, suburbs, and rural areas. In the past, men were far more likely to be drinkers than women, with male alcoholics outnumbering female alcoholics by four or five to one. But as women have begun to participate more fully in other aspects of working and social life, they have also begun to catch up in both social and problem drinking. In some areas, such as the Miami region, nearly half of the alcoholics are now estimated to be women. (It is possible that the differences in the past were not really as great as they seemed. A housewife, spending most of the day alone and unobserved in her own home, could much more easily hide an alcohol problem than a man exposed to the view of others for most of the day in an office or factory.)

Unmarried people are more likely to drink than married people, and young adults show a higher proportion of drinkers than people over forty (though some studies indicate the proportion of *heavy* drinkers reaches a peak in the forty-five to forty-nine age range). All the widely practiced religions frown on drunkenness; many Protestant sects that preached abstinence at one time have switched to an emphasis on moderation. Still, the highest proportions of drinkers are found among Catholics, Episcopalians, and Jews, although Jews have a lower-than-average percentage of heavy drinkers. Churchgoers and nonchurchgoers have about the same proportions of nondrinkers, although nonchurchgoers are more likely to be heavy drinkers than churchgoers.

Why do people drink? For some, alcoholic beverages seem a fitting way to celebrate special events, from a wedding to signing an important contract. ("Let's have a drink on that!") For some, wine is a part of religious rituals. Some people regularly drink alcoholic beverages with meals, and consider them part of their normal diet. Some find alcoholic beverages relaxing, a way to unwind after a long, hard day.

Some people feel that a drink before dinner helps to stimulate the appetite. The relaxing effect of alcohol may indeed make a meal more enjoyable, but it may not be an unmixed blessing: some studies indicate that alcohol tends to dull the taste buds.

Some use alcohol as a "social lubricant," permitting them to lose their shyness and inhibitions and enjoy themselves at parties. This effect of alcohol has been found to depend greatly on the social setting and on people's expectations. In experimental studies, people at parties were given rum-flavored water, or fruit punch that had not been "spiked" with alcohol, and told that they were drinking alcoholic beverages. Most of the people behaved just as though they had really had a few drinks of alcohol.

The widespread practice of offering alcohol as a sign of hospitality causes many people to accept a drink simply because it seems the courteous thing to do. At parties, pressure may be put on the nondrinker to join in and not "spoil the fun." Studies of people's responses with and without alcohol have shown that drinkers tend to laugh uproariously at cartoons that nondrinkers may not find particularly funny. Jokes told by someone who has had a few drinks may seem hilariously funny to others who have been drinking but fall flat for someone who has not had any alcohol. So the nondrinker in a social situation may be made to feel like a wet blanket. On the other hand, some nondrinkers abstain in such an unpleasant and aggressive way that they make everyone else feel guilty.

Some people drink because they like the taste of alcoholic beverages. Most people find the taste of alcohol unpleasant at first, but they may go on drinking because they enjoy the effects of alcohol. Later they may acquire a taste for alcoholic drinks.

For some, drinking is associated with sophistication and affluence. Connoisseurs of fine wines and distilled spirits learn about the various types of alcoholic beverages and develop their palates so that they can taste small differences between different brands and vintages. For connoisseurs, drinking becomes an intellectual pleasure, and they may also be rewarded by the admiration of others.

For young people, the desire to feel mature and share in adult activities may be a motivation for drinking. Or teenagers may drink as a form of rebellion, either against their parents or against laws they feel to be unfair and hypocritical. The lure of "forbidden fruit" may make alcohol attractive.

In our culture, most of these reasons for social drinking are considered a part of appropriate drinking behavior. Of course, social drinking can lead to inappropriate behavior if alcohol is used to excess and results in drunkenness or violence. But some forms of drinking are frowned upon because they may be signs of a drinking problem. Drinking alone and drinking in the morning are commonly regarded as unacceptable behavior. Gulping drinks to bring on the feeling of intoxication faster may be another danger sign. People who use alcohol regularly as a crutch to help them forget their problems may find themselves becoming increasingly dependent on alcohol and consuming more and more—until ultimately drinking becomes a focus of their lives and they drink for the sake of drinking rather than for social purposes.

The prevailing views of appropriate and inappropriate drinking behavior have grown up out of a complex mixture of ethnic backgrounds. The population of the United States has been built up by a series of waves of immigrants from various countries, religions, and social classes. They brought with them typical ways of looking at things and handling life's situations. A number of studies have been made of the attitudes of various ethnic groups toward alcohol, both to gain insight into how the typically American view was formed (and is continuing to evolve) and in the hope of finding some hints on ways of coping with the problem of alcoholism. The groups that have been studied most often have been the Italians, the Jews, the Irish, and the Chinese, for these groups have been characterized by consistent but quite different attitudes toward alcohol.

For the Italians, wine is the beverage of choice, and it has traditionally been drunk with meals, within the family group. Everyone drinks, as a matter of course. Very young children drink milk, but somewhat older children drink diluted wine. As they grow, the concentration of the wine is increased, until they share the beverage of the older family members. Drinking is nearly universal, but it is controlled in several ways— both by the family setting, and by the practice of eating while drinking, which tends to dilute the effects of alcohol on the body. An episode of drunkenness in a young person who is just learning to drink is generally shrugged off as one of the common hazards of growing up. But repeated drunkenness in older people is severely frowned upon, and alcohol abuse has traditionally been rare. (In modern Italy, however, according to the latest studies, the traditional controls seem to be breaking down; cases of cirrhosis of the liver and other aspects of problem drinking are on the rise.)

Among Orthodox Jews, wine is an important part of the religious ritual. Wine is drunk by the whole family to welcome the Sabbath each week, and wine is used in various festivals. Alcoholic beverages are also used on social occasions, but again in a family setting and in moderation. Drunkenness is frowned upon, as reflecting badly not only on the individual but on the whole group. As a result, Jews have traditionally had a high proportion of drinkers, but a very low proportion of heavy drinkers. Since the last large waves of Jewish immigration, in the late 1800s and early 1900s, there has been a growing tendency for many Jews to become assimilated into the general population, adopting the prevailing American customs in many areas of life, including drinking practices. As a result, alcoholism among Jews is not quite the rarity it once was.

However, it is still considerably below the average. As one Jewish psychiatrist put it, only half-jokingly, "Jews don't drink when they have problems, they *eat!*"

The Chinese have traditionally been a very family-centered culture, with ties extending to a broader group of relatives. A strong emphasis is placed on the welfare of the group. The traditional Chinese attitude toward alcohol fits into this framework. Alcoholic beverages are accepted as one of the physical pleasures of life and are enjoyed without the conflicting emotions that many other peoples attach to them. Heavy drinking is acceptable, though the manly ideal is to drink a great deal *without* showing signs of intoxication. Members of the community show a protective attitude toward a person who may become incapacitated by alcohol. But consequences of drinking that might harm the group, particularly aggressive behavior, are strongly disapproved and penalized. As a result, though drinking is common, problem drinking is rare among Chinese-Americans.

The Irish, by contrast, are an ethnic group in which both heavy drinking and alcoholism are especially frequent. The reasons for this drinking pattern may be found in the background of the Irish immigrants. In rural Ireland, periodic crop failures and lean times meant that often there was barely enough food available to stay alive. Farms were small and crowded and were worked by an extended family, including the grandparents, the farmer and his wife, and their unmarried sons and daughters. One son inherited the farm, while the other children eventually left, the girls usually to marry or become nuns and the boys to become priests or apprentices in a trade, or to emigrate. Until the father was willing to give up running the farm, his sons were treated as "boys," and they often had to delay marrying for many years. Under these conditions, drink rather than food was the customary mark of hospitality. In addition, the men would often visit an inn or public house to drink. Drinking bouts marked holidays, business meetings, weddings and wakes, and practically every other conceivable occasion. A bit of "poteen" helped to dull the hunger pangs (supplying some of the calories that were missing from the restricted diet) and ease worries. Drinking was recognized as a way to release the resentment that built up among the "boys" against their elders. Drunkenness and aggressive behavior were not generally frowned upon, unless a man's drinking habit began to endanger the family's finances. In America, popular attitudes toward drunkenness and brawling were less indulgent; but the traditions of gay carousing, buying rounds of drinks for one's companions, and the use of alcohol as an escape from personal problems persisted among Irish immigrants.

The attitude toward drinking most typical in America today tends to accept drinking in moderate amounts, for social purposes. Yet problem drinking and alcohol dependence are on the rise. Some people have blamed the tensions and complexity of modern living —for some it seems impossible to face the problems of each new day without some sort of "chemical crutch." Automation has reduced many jobs to a dull routine that prompts many workers to seek stimulation elsewhere. Yet our highly technological, mechanized way of life often demands a high degree of mental and physical control. A factory worker who keeps a bottle in his locker to tide him over the day's dull routine may cause an accident as a result of slowed reactions and impaired judgment. And driving a car in modern traffic requires such a high degree of coordination, skill, and constant split-second decision making that alcohol all too often makes a fatal difference.

Drinking and Driving

What if everyone in the stands watching a World Series game—fifty thousand people—were suddenly to die? This would be recorded as one of the greatest tragedies of all time. And yet, each year about fifty thousand Americans are killed in driving accidents. For each person who is killed, another forty or so are injured in traffic accidents—so that altogether, you stand about one chance in one hundred of being injured or killed in a traffic accident during the next year.

With a public health problem this great, it is natural that driving accidents have been the object of intensive study. Researchers have been trying to find out what factors are most likely to cause accidents, in the hope of working out ways to reduce the toll of death and injuries. Many factors are involved—a driver of a car on a highway or in crowded city traffic must expertly maneuver a ton of sophisticated machinery

69

according to a complicated set of rules and regulations, meanwhile observing and anticipating the actions of other drivers, whose vehicles may be separated from his by only feet or even inches. The physical condition of both the car and the driver, the driver's intelligence, experience, emotional balance, and ability to note and react to the sometimes erratic and unexpected behavior of pedestrians and other drivers all play a role in his success in avoiding accidents. Considering the complex skills involved in driving and the effects that alcohol can have on the body and brain, it is not surprising that drinking has been implicated as a major factor in our highway death toll.

Three main types of studies have contributed to our knowledge of the hazards of mixing drinking and driving. Tests of volunteers have measured the effects of alcohol on abilities and skills presumed to be important in driving. Other studies have been conducted in actual test vehicles, on specially designed obstacle courses. Statistical studies of the involvement of alcohol in actual accidents have helped to complete the picture.

Hundreds of laboratory experiments on volunteer drinkers have revealed a consistent pattern. After one typical drink of distilled spirits or two bottles of beer, raising the blood alcohol level to about 0.03 percent, there is little or no detectable effect. But beginning with a blood alcohol level around 0.05 percent, characteristic signs of impairment begin to show up. The efficiency of vision and hearing is reduced. The ability to respond to stimulation when objects pass into the field of vision from the sides is especially affected—the drinker suffers from a sort of "tunnel vision." The speed of reaction is slowed, a result that has important consequences in driving at high speeds. Even under the best of circumstances, a brief time elapses between a driver's noting an emergency that requires braking, the decision to do so, and the transmitting of the decision to the driver's leg muscles, which carry out the act. During this time, the car continues to move, and it travels a further distance while the brakes are bringing it to a halt. Under the influence of alcohol, the crucial time lag in reacting is lengthened, and important feet may be added to the car's stopping distance. The drinker's attention span is shortened, and his muscle coordination is reduced. Higher mental abilities, involving judgment and the ability to organize past experiences quickly, are impaired. There may be changes in what the drinker sees or thinks he sees, and he may tend to take risky chances that he would not take while sober. The drinker's performance of tasks requiring concentration becomes erratic. Meanwhile, the euphoria induced by alcohol may make a drinker believe that he is doing better than usual and prevent him from compensating for his impaired abilities.

Studies on devices that simulate driving situations and actual test drives support the findings of these laboratory studies. In the range of blood alcohol levels from 0.05 percent to 0.10 percent, the degree of impairment varies. Some people may seem relatively unaffected—particularly the most experienced drinkers and/or the most experienced drivers, who are able to compensate for the effects of alcohol. Other people may show some signs of impairment even below 0.05 percent. But when blood alcohol levels rise above 0.15 percent, everyone shows a pronounced impairment of mental and physical abilities. In all cases the impairment is greatest when the blood alcohol is rising, soon after drinking.

Studies of actual traffic accidents in which people were killed have generally shown that either the driver responsible or the victim (another driver or a pedestrian) or both had substantial blood alcohol levels in about 50 percent of the cases. In some respects this is not surprising. About 80 percent of the adult population of the United States are licensed drivers, and about two-thirds of adults drink. There must necessarily be many people who are both drivers and drinkers, and sometimes they may drive after drinking.

There is not much information available about how many people drink, then drive, and are *not* involved in accidents. In one study, conducted in Grand Rapids, Michigan, information was gathered on 5985 drivers who had been involved in accidents. Then 7590 additional drivers who happened to be passing the site of previous accidents under similar conditions (on the same day of the week, at the same time of day, etc.) were stopped and tested for alcohol. Eighteen times as many drivers in the accident group had blood alcohol concentrations above 0.15 percent as in the group of randomly selected drivers. For the 0.10–0.15 percent range, there was a fourfold difference, while for 0.05 to 0.10 percent, there were twice as many among the drivers who had accidents.

In another study, two-thirds of the alcohol-related accidents were found to involve a driver who was a problem drinker, defined in the study as a driver with a blood alcohol level above 0.25 percent, or one who had a past history of alcoholism or previous arrests for offenses involving alcohol.

Most states have now adopted a scale setting 0.10 percent blood alcohol as the level indicating impairment. Values in the range from 0.05 to 0.10 percent are legally admissible as evidence of possible impairment, while values below 0.05 percent are evidence that a person is not legally under the influence of alcohol.

In fatal accidents, the blood alcohol levels are routinely determined directly in blood samples from the victims. But live drivers stopped by police officers on suspicion of being under the influence of alcohol often resist the idea of permitting a blood specimen to be taken. The courts have generally upheld the idea that taking blood samples without a person's consent is an infringement of his civil rights. As a result, alcohol analyses are usually made on a device such as a Drunkometer or Breathalyzer, in which a sample of the suspect's breath passes over chemicals that show a specific color reaction with alcohol. The alcohol concentration in the breath is proportional to that in the blood, and the results are converted to blood alcohol values.

An interesting sidelight to the Breathalyzer tests has recently been discovered. It has been found that lemon drops and certain soft drinks contain aldehydes, which affect the crystals in the Breathalyzer in the same way as alcohol. A driver stopped by a state trooper just after sucking lemon drops might show a positive test, even though he had not been drinking. Fortunately, the test remains positive only as long as the aldehydes remain in the saliva, for about fifteen minutes.

It is generally agreed that drinking before (or during) driving is a major contributing factor in accidents—perhaps the most frequent one. But a more complicated problem is deciding what to do about it. It would be ideal if everyone followed the slogan "If you drive, don't drink, and if you drink, don't drive." But sometimes there seems to be no practical alternative. People may drink at restaurants or parties from which the only available means of transportation is the automobile. An occasional social drinker, for example, who may drive home after a few drinks at a wedding, does not think of himself as a "drunken driver," and he may be appalled if he is stopped on the highway by a police officer, subjected to a Breathalyzer test, and has his driver's license automatically suspended for several months or more because he was legally "driving under the influence." In today's commuter society, such an occurrence might mean the loss of a person's job and great hardships to his or her family. Yet studies have shown that chronic problem drinkers, who are responsible for such a disproportionate share of traffic deaths, often ignore even the harshest penalties. The Department of Transportation estimates that about 80 percent of drivers whose licenses have been suspended or revoked for repeated drunken driving offenses go on driving without a license.

In a number of communities, efforts are being made to identify problem drinkers before they are involved in fatal accidents and steer them into rehabilitation programs. For the social drinker, a program such as the one established in New Orleans may be useful. A van equipped with Breathalyzer facilities has been set up. People who have been drinking may voluntarily take the test, and if they have a blood alcohol level above 0.10 percent they are offered rides home. Perhaps the best hope for the future may lie in the laboratory, in research efforts to devise a "sobering pill" which will permit drinkers to enjoy their alcohol at social occasions and get home safely afterward.

Teenage Drinking

In some ways, our present laws prohibiting teenage drinking are quite unreasonable. It is illegal to sell or serve alcoholic beverages to minors, yet we expect young people to take their places suddenly at eighteen or twenty-one in an adult culture where drinking is the norm. Somehow, miraculously, without any practice, they are supposed to know how to drink sensibly and appropriately.

Fortunately or unfortunately, all the studies of what teenagers actually do, rather than what they are supposed to, show that teenagers do drink. The percentage of teenage drinkers increases steadily with age, until at eighteen the proportion of drinkers is approximately the same as in the adult population—i.e., about two-thirds of eighteen-year-olds drink at least occasionally. The percentage of teenage drinkers varies depending on the region of the country. One study, which showed 86 percent teenage drinkers in Nassau

County, New York, and only 44 percent in rural Kansas, was typical of the general trend: teenagers in metropolitan areas are more likely to drink than those in rural regions. Boys, who are traditionally given more freedom than girls, have a higher percentage of drinkers than girls. The difference is especially pronounced in rural areas, and it decreases with age.

The majority of teenagers drink infrequently. In one survey, teenagers who stated that they had had an alcoholic beverage within the past week ranged from 11 to 43 percent of the total—in other words, the majority had not had anything to drink for at least a week. Yet regular heavy drinking is a growing problem among young people: a 1974 special report to the U. S. Congress on Alcohol and Health noted that about 5 percent of teenagers surveyed reported that they get drunk or very high at least once a week. The percentage increases steadily with age: for high school seniors it is nearly 10 percent.

Beer is the most commonly consumed alcoholic beverage among young people. Wine is second, and hard liquor last.

Most teenagers who drink do so in their own home, or in the homes of friends, often under their parents' supervision. Drinking at parties is another frequent practice. Studies of changes in teenage drinking practices after the legal age is passed show an understandable jump in the percentage of drinking in bars and other public places, and a sharp drop in drinking in inappropriate places such as parked cars.

It is a popular impression that teenagers drink mainly as a form of rebellion. In some cases this may be true. But more often, drinking teenagers are imitating the behavior of the adults in their community, and drinking is viewed as a way of feeling mature. Indeed, parents have more of an effect on teenage drinking attitudes and practices than they sometimes realize. One study of college students attempted to determine the relative importance of various influences on a person's decision to drink or not. Among male students who had been advised by their parents not to drink, 40 percent abstained. Only 18 percent of those who received no advice abstained. Advice from the church or school seemed to have a reverse effect: for those who received such advice only from their church, only 16 percent abstained, and all but 10 percent of those who were advised to abstain only in school went on to drink anyway.

Parents have mixed feelings about teenagers' drinking. Often, of course, it is the parents themselves who have introduced their children to alcohol, believing that it is better for them to learn how to drink properly under supervised conditions. When parents learn that their child has been drinking surreptitiously, their reaction often may be, "Thank goodness! We were afraid he was on drugs!" Yet many parents do worry about teenagers and alcohol, especially in the areas of drunkenness, sex, and driving.

To some degree, these fears are justified, for alcohol holds special pitfalls for teenagers. Among the factors influencing the speed and degree of intoxication that a given amount of alcohol can produce, teenagers have two strikes against them. Usually their body weight is lower than that of adults, and thus they cannot "hold" as much liquor. And teenagers lack the experience in drinking that would permit them to compensate for changes in coordination, judgment, and mental control. Inexperience and unfamiliarity with various kinds of alcoholic beverages may also cause teenagers to underestimate the potency of a drink, and they may overindulge accidentally.

Adolescence is a time of many adjustments, and many teenagers often feel troubled and confused. They are painfully acquiring experience in social situations, and may often feel ill at ease. Alcohol may seem to offer easy answers to these problems. A few drinks may relieve inhibitions and make it easier to relate to others in social situations. Alcohol may relieve worries about schoolwork and future careers and may smooth away feelings of failure and frustration. But the teenager who comes to depend on alcohol in order to forget problems will not learn how to work through them constructively. The teenager who depends on alcohol to feel relaxed on dates and at parties will not have a chance to develop social skills and may come to feel that he or she can't have a good time without drinking.

Teenagers, like adults, sometimes are stimulated sexually by alcohol and may find themselves kissing, petting, or having intercourse under circumstances when they would have restrained themselves while sober. With the easing of inhibitions and blurring of judgment that alcohol brings, sex acts are more likely to be begun impulsively, without taking any precautions for contraception. And thus both pregnancy and venereal diseases become very real possibilities.

Drinking and driving are a particularly potent mix for teenagers. They tend to be not only inexperienced drinkers but also inexperienced drivers, without the reserves of judgment and reflexes that years of driving experience develop. Traffic accidents are the leading cause of death in the 15 to 24 age group, and accidents involving a teenage driver who had been drinking tend to receive a great deal of publicity. But fortunately the vast majority of teenagers do behave responsibly in both drinking and driving.

What Is Alcoholism?

Where do you draw the line between social drinking and problem drinking, and between problem drinking and alcoholism? There is a great deal of confusion and controversy today about alcoholism—not only about what causes it and how it should be treated, but even about exactly what conditions should be regarded as alcoholism. A member of the Women's Christian Temperance Union might say that anyone who drinks alcoholic beverages—no matter what kind, how often, how much, or for what reasons—is an alcoholic, for anyone who has started to drink has embarked on a road that will inevitably lead downward to the depths of despair and degradation. At the other end of the spectrum, people often think of an alcoholic as being a Skid Row derelict, an unwashed bum either cadging dimes and quarters for the next bottle of cheap wine or passed out in the gutter. Yet most people in the field of alcohol problems today recognize that far from all drinkers are alcoholics, and that indeed most social drinkers will never become alcoholics. (Estimates of the number of drinkers who become alcoholics range from 5 to 10 percent.) And even among alcoholics, the great majority manage to hang on to their jobs and to some semblance of normal life. The true Skid Row types account for only about 3 to 5 percent of alcoholics.

Characteristics of alcoholics recognized by many people in the field are: first, an inability to choose consistently whether to drink or not to drink; then, once a drink has been taken, an inability to choose consistently whether to continue drinking or to stop. Alcoholics feel that they *need* to drink, and they go on drinking even when their reason and judgment tell them to stop.

Other signs of alcoholism are the harmful effects of a person's drinking practices on himself and others. The alcoholic's health may suffer; alcoholics may become unreliable at work, jeopardizing their jobs or even endangering the lives and safety of others; they may become difficult to live with, making their families miserable and possibly breaking up their marriages. An alcoholic is aware of these effects and may want to stop drinking—may even promise to stop drinking—but he or she does not stop.

Drinking itself becomes a focus of the alcoholic's life. It is not a pleasant accompaniment to other activities. Instead, drinking is a goal in itself. A large fraction of an alcoholic's energies is directed toward looking forward to the next drink, arranging to obtain alcohol, and possibly concealing his or her drinking and its effects.

Is alcoholism an addiction? This is a point on which there is still some disagreement. In some ways alcohol acts as an addictive drug. Steady drinkers become habituated to alcohol and gradually find that they must drink larger and larger amounts to achieve the same effect. And if drinking is suddenly stopped after a period of heavy alcohol consumption, there are withdrawal symptoms—nausea, tremors, hallucinations, and even convulsions resembling epileptic seizures. Delirium tremens, the most severe form of withdrawal, which occurs after several days of abstinence following a long period of heavy drinking, is more serious than the withdrawal symptoms associated with heroin and other narcotics. Delirium tremens is actually fatal in about 10 percent of the cases.

But in some ways alcohol is not a typical "addictive drug." Most habitual drinkers do not become addicted to alcohol. Cases of "instant addiction" to alcohol (developing after a single use or only a few) have been reported, but they are rare. Usually alcoholism develops gradually and progressively, over a period of five years or more. And alcoholism seems to be a far more complicated condition than just a physical reaction of the body. A whole complex of psychological attitudes toward drinking and toward the person's problems and relationships with others are also involved. Many experts in the field prefer to emphasize the aspect of psychological dependence—the feeling of "needing" a drink, of turning to alcohol to ease tensions and forget about problems that cannot be faced head-on—rather than the idea of physical addiction.

With all the confusion even among experts about what alcoholism is, it is not surprising that alcoholics themselves often do not think of themselves as alcoholics, do not realize that they have a serious drinking problem. The National Institute on Alcohol Abuse and Alcoholism of the U. S. Department of Health, Education, and Welfare suggests the following quiz to help suspected alcoholics recognize their problem:

1. Do you think and talk about drinking often?
2. Do you drink more now than you used to?
3. Do you sometimes gulp drinks?
4. Do you often take a drink to help you relax?
5. Do you drink when you are alone?

6. Do you sometimes forget what happened while you were drinking?

7. Do you keep a bottle hidden somewhere—at home or at work—for quick pick-me-ups?

8. Do you need a drink to have fun?

9. Do you ever just start drinking without really thinking about it?

10. Do you drink in the morning to relieve a hangover?

Answering yes to at least four of these ten questions is a danger sign that an alcohol problem may exist. Another typical list of problem signs is cited by Alcoholics Anonymous:

Many alcoholics find that only alcohol can make them feel self-confident and at ease with other people;

—they often want "just one more" at the end of a party;

—they look forward to drinking occasions and think about them a lot;

—they get drunk when they had not planned to;

—they try to control their drinking by changing types of liquor, going on the wagon, or taking pledges;

—they sneak drinks;

—they lie about their drinking, hide bottles;

—they drink at work or in school;

—they drink alone;

—they have blackouts, periods during a drinking occasion of which they have no memory the following day;

—they drink in the morning;

—they fail to eat properly and become malnourished;

—they develop cirrhosis of the liver;

—they shake violently, hallucinate, or have convulsions when withdrawn from liquor.

Many people seeing lists such as these seize upon one or two items that do not apply to them and sigh with relief, "*I'm* not an alcoholic—I never drink before 3 P.M."—or never drink liquor, only beer or wine; or never drink alone. But alcoholism is a very individual condition. The form it takes in a particular person depends on many things—the individual's body reaction to alcohol, personality and way of looking at things, family background, etc.

Alcoholism is a progressive condition. A person is not suddenly transformed overnight from a social drinker into an alcoholic; the symptoms of alcoholism appear gradually, rather than all at once. Doctors and researchers recognize several phases in the development of alcoholism.

In the first phase, the drinker begins to drink more often, and more at a time. Perhaps before he or she drank only on social occasions, to "loosen up" and become more relaxed and convivial. But now more occasions become drinking occasions, and the main motivation for drinking is the "high" the alcohol brings, or the easing of problems that seem too painful to face. More and more alcohol is needed to bring the same "high." At this stage the developing alcoholic may begin to experience blackouts. The day after an occasion of heavy drinking, he will be completely unable to recall what he said or did during a particular period. It is as though the drinker's memory were a tape recorder, and when he tries to replay a certain part of the tape, it is a total blank. Yet people who were with the drinker at the time say that he behaved apparently quite normally. He did not even seem drunk at the time—he talked, walked without staggering, and may even have driven a car, all apparently in full control. Only now he cannot remember any of it.

During this first stage of alcoholism, there may be no apparent changes in the alcoholic's personality, even though he or she is drinking increasing amounts of alcohol. At work or school, in family life, the dependent drinker appears to be functioning quite normally. A businessman, for example, may be settled in a routine of steady drinking—a couple of martinis at lunch, two more before dinner, wine during dinner, an after-dinner liqueur, and perhaps a "nightcap" to help him sleep. Then he breaks his leg, is sent to the hospital where he does not receive his regular supply of alcohol, and a couple of days later is astonished to find himself seized by an attack of D.T.'s.

In the middle phase of alcoholism, a person drinks not for social reasons but because he has to, in order to maintain physical and emotional equilibrium. Once he takes a drink, he cannot stop, even though he knows that he may make a fool of himself or drink until he passes out. Alcoholics Anonymous members describe the feeling, "One drink is too many, and a hundred is never enough." The blissful "high" that the alcoholic remembers often eludes him, and he drinks more and more in a vain attempt to recapture it. At this stage, the alcoholic's personality begins to change. He may lie about his drinking, or conceal it, or think up elaborate justifications for drinking and fanciful explanations for his behavior. The alcoholic lives more and more in a fantasy world and may be full of plans for future achievements that seem unrealistic to those around him. He wakes up in the morning feeling physically miserable, but a drink makes him feel better. So he makes up alibis about his drinking and fights attempts to help him stop—he sees these as a threat to take away the only "medicine" he has found that can help him.

During the middle phase of alcoholism, a person can still function reasonably well. But his increasing unreliability and unpredictable behavior make it more and more difficult to hold a job and may gradually turn the alcoholic's family and friends against him. He may behave aggressively toward people around him, and later be remorseful. He may try to "make it up" to his family and others he has hurt by spending irresponsibly on gifts for them. He may promise to give alcohol up, and he may keep his promise for weeks or even months—but then he relapses. Drinking episodes may lead to hospitalization, but often the official diagnosis will be gastritis ("stomach problems") or some other ailment which is more socially acceptable than alcoholism. The doctor may not realize that a patient has a drinking problem, or may try to shield the alcoholic and his family.

In the last stage of alcoholism, the alcoholic is often intoxicated for long periods of time. He will do things to obtain alcohol—steal, or write bad checks—that he would not normally have done. If he cannot get a supply of alcoholic beverages, he will drink anything that may be intoxicating—cough medicine, vanilla extract, rubbing alcohol. He neglects his eating, and deficiency diseases become pronounced. Signs of brain and liver damage may appear. The alcoholic develops persistent tremors or shakes and is unable to do the simplest things—tying his shoes, opening a can, for example—without taking a drink first. His life—job, family—is falling apart. At this point, abandoning his complicated system of rationalizations about his drinking, the alcoholic may seek help, and a more or less complete recovery (depending on the amount of physical damage years of heavy drinking have produced) is still possible. Or the chronic alcoholic may "drop out" of normal life entirely. Ultimately he may literally drink himself to death.

Not all alcoholics go through all the typical stages of alcoholism in precisely the same order, or show all of the characteristic symptoms. There seem to be two main patterns of alcohol abuse: the steady drinker, who drinks perhaps a pint of whiskey or more every day; and the spree drinker, who alternates long periods of sobriety, lasting weeks or months, with drinking binges, days or weeks of drunkenness. Studies have shown that in France, where alcoholic beverages are considered an acceptable daily drink for everyone, even children, the typical alcoholic is a steady drinker. French alcoholics have fewer incidents of drunkenness (they are more likely to drink wine, with a lower alcohol content) and less difficulty with families or trouble with the police. But they have a high rate of cirrhosis of the liver (ten times the rate in the United States) and other physical damages caused by alcohol. In the United States, on the other hand, periodic "benders" or drinking sprees are a more common life-style for alcoholics, and incidents of drunkenness are frequent. In one survey of hospitalized American alcoholics, less than 10 percent denied that they had had spells of prolonged drunkenness, while 71 percent of a similar group of French alcoholics made this denial.

What causes alcoholism? Some specialists in the field tend to stress the aspect of psychological dependence. Alcoholics, they say, are unable to cope with the stresses and strains of everyday living, and they have developed the habit of relying on alcohol to relieve stresses. Yet why do they turn to alcohol, rather than to other drugs or to other approaches such as mystical or religious experiences? Perhaps because alcohol is a readily available, legal substance that most people are introduced to in the course of normal social life. Or perhaps the reasons lie deep in the alcoholic's subconscious mind, in past experiences hidden even from himself. It is sometimes stated that alcoholics "lack willpower," and if they would only try hard enough, they could control their habit. Yet in the early and middle stages of alcoholism, alcoholics often show a high degree of willpower, carefully limiting their consumption of alcohol even when their bodies are craving for more. Efforts have been made to draw up a picture of the "alcoholic personality," to spot people who might have a high risk of becoming alcoholics. But such attempts have not been very successful—the alcoholic personality profiles that have been devised usually also fit many people who never become alcoholics. Studies of ethnic backgrounds and social attitudes toward drinking have been of some value, but they do not tell the whole story.

More and more, alcoholism has begun to be regarded as a disease, with physical bases that may ultimately be discovered and treated. This attitude was recognized by the medical community in 1956, when the American Medical Association officially declared alcoholism to be a disease. Many doctors and other workers in the field of alcoholism objected to this decision, saying that if alcoholics were told that their condition was a physical condition, beyond their control, they would not work to cure themselves. But others pointed out that the situation is similar to that of patients with diabetes, high blood pressure, or some other condition that requires a program of regular treatment over a period of many years. It would be both cruel and foolish to tell such patients that they are morally to blame for their condition, yet recognizing it as a disease does not absolve them from working to follow their diet, take their medicine regularly, and cooperate with their doctors in the treatment. Regarding alcoholism as a disease has opened up many promising lines of research into its causes and treatment.

One question that arises is: Is alcoholism, or a tendency to alcoholism, hereditary? It is a common observation that alcoholism tends to run in families. Studies have shown that children of heavy drinkers are much more likely to be heavy drinkers themselves than children of moderate drinkers or nondrinkers. And children of nondrinkers are likely to be nondrinkers as well. (But when children of nondrinkers do begin to drink, they have a higher-than-average risk of becoming alcoholics. It is theorized that without a background of family examples of how to drink sensibly, these people are more likely to lose control when they do drink—in other words, social factors are important, too.) Yet even studies indicating that children of alcoholics have a high risk of becoming alcoholics do not necessarily indicate that heredity is involved. Perhaps it is merely the example of using alcohol to cope with problems that is at work here.

Some studies have tried to separate the effects of

heredity and environment. Donald Goodwin, a psychiatrist at Washington University, in St. Louis, Missouri, made a study of half-brothers. He found that if the father in a family was an alcoholic, his real sons had a high risk of becoming alcoholics. But boys raised by an alcoholic stepfather were no more likely to become alcoholics than the general population. Children of an alcoholic parent raised in a nonalcoholic family were six times as likely to become alcoholics as those whose natural parents did not have a drinking problem. Other studies of identical twins raised apart, some in homes with an alcoholic parent, others away from the alcoholic parent, also seem to support the idea that heredity plays an important role. Dr. Goodwin suggests that what is inherited might be differences in the effect alcohol has on the body and brain; some people would not become alcoholics because alcohol makes them sick, or does not do much for them emotionally.

Researchers are searching for physical differences between people who become alcoholics and those who do not—differences in the metabolism (the chemical reactions of the body) and especially in the chemicals of the brain. Some studies, for example, have shown that alcoholics have an abnormally high requirement for certain B vitamins, and alcoholism has also been found to be linked with hypoglycemia (low blood sugar). Yet the problem with such studies is that it is impossible to determine whether the differences found in alcoholics' bodies are causes or effects of alcoholism. Does a person turn to alcohol because his body is craving something to satisfy a deficiency, or does the deficiency develop as a result of changes in the body caused by years of heavy drinking? Such questions can always be asked about studies of people who are alcoholics already. Yet an alcoholism researcher who wanted to study people *before* they develop the condition couldn't know in advance which members of the "normal" population would be destined to become alcoholics, and massive screening studies on humans take many years and are enormously expensive.

One solution to this dilemma has been the development of animal studies. A mouse is not a man. It is much smaller (and therefore is affected by much smaller amounts of various drugs and other chemicals). A mouse "lives faster" than a human—its heartbeat is faster, its body temperature is higher, it matures in just a month or two, and its life span is far shorter than a man's. It also has a number of unique body reactions that are not shared by humans, and vice versa. A mouse can make its own vitamin C, for example, while a human cannot and must obtain this necessary substance in food. So there are definite limitations on how far findings from experiments on mice and other laboratory animals can be extended to humans. But there are many basic similarities, too—enough so that much important information about how our own bodies work, in health and disease, has been discovered first through experiments on animals.

Animals do not usually drink alcohol willingly. However, by generations of careful breeding, scientists have produced strains of mice and rats that actually prefer alcohol to water. These rodents will even work for their drinks, pressing a lever in their cage to receive a ration of alcohol. Experiments on alcoholic miniature pigs have also been conducted, at the University of Missouri's Sinclair Comparative Medical Research Farm. Like their human counterparts, these 120-pound pigs get drunk on vodka, staggering and falling down. Some pigs tend to drink more alcohol than others when they are supplied with all the vodka they want to drink. Like people, the pigs have individual reactions to alcohol—some become sleepy, while others become aggressive. If their supply of alcohol is suddenly cut off, the miniature pigs suffer withdrawal symptoms very similar to those of human alcoholics; some of the pigs in the experiment died during withdrawal.

Animal studies of alcoholism are beginning to yield some very intriguing results. Liise Ahtee, a pharmacologist at the University of Helsinki in Finland, reports that the brains of rats bred to prefer alcohol to water have a 15 to 20 percent higher concentration of serotonin, an important nerve transmitter chemical that helps brain cells to function, than the brains of normal rats. This difference is observed in the alcoholic-prone rats even when they have never been given any alcohol to drink—it is not an effect of alcohol, but a hereditary trait. When such rats are allowed to drink as much ethyl alcohol (in a 10 percent solution) as they wish for a month, their serotonin level rises even higher, to 31 percent above the normal level. Yet if rats from a nonalcoholic line are forced to drink the same amount of alcohol as the alcoholic rats drink voluntarily, there is no change in the nonalcoholic rats' brain serotonin levels.

Of course, there is a great difference between a rat's brain and the human brain, although serotonin plays a similar important role in both. Perhaps the difference found in the alcoholic rats' brains may not apply to man. But rhesus monkeys are much closer to humans. At Purdue University, Robert D. Myers worked with both rats and rhesus monkeys, injecting tiny amounts of alcohol directly into their brains. When the animals were offered a free choice of alcohol or water, at first they chose water. But after a few weeks of alcohol injections, the rats and monkeys suddenly began to choose alcohol. Soon they were steady drinkers. Then they were given a drug called parachlorophenylalanine (PCPA), which is known to lower the level of serotonin in the brain. Almost immediately the addicted animals began to drink less alcohol. Even after the drug was stopped, the formerly alcoholic animals remained "moderate" drinkers, drinking much less alcohol than a similar group that had not received PCPA.

Animal experiments such as these are not only providing information on possible causes of alcoholism but are also suggesting possible treatments for this disease.

Treating the Alcoholic

For many years, alcoholism was commonly viewed as a moral lapse, rather than a disease. It was thought that the appropriate treatment for public drunkenness was to arrest drunkards and place them in the "drunk tank" of the local jail until they "dried out." But this policy accomplished little toward reaching the causes of the problem. For some, the humiliation of being arrested and locked up in jail provided the spark for a decision to stop drinking. But many alcoholics would soon be back in jail again, within a few days, weeks, or months. The pattern would be repeated over and over again, so often that the public policy of jailing alcoholics has sometimes been referred to as a "revolving door" policy.

As the idea that alcoholism is a treatable disease became more widely accepted, many communities began to eliminate their laws on drunkenness, or at least not to enforce them. Now it is usually considered more appropriate to try to steer the repeating "drunk and disorderly" offender into a treatment program.

Treating an alcoholic is a long and often discouraging process. Alcoholism is more than a physical sickness; it includes a whole complex of psychological motives and attitudes. The alcoholic may not wholeheartedly want to get well. The idea of facing life without the comfort of alcohol may seem terrifying. Over a period of years an alcoholic may have drifted into a circle of friends who are all heavy drinkers too, and he may feel that he would have nothing in common with anyone else if he quit drinking. The prospect of life without alcohol may seem dull and empty.

It was thought at one time that an alcoholic could not be treated successfully until he or she had "hit bottom"—lost job and family, was broke and perhaps in jail. Now the feeling is that just as alcoholism is a very individual disease, "hitting bottom" may mean many different things to different people. For one man it may be the sudden realization that he cannot function until he has his morning "pick-me-up." For one woman it may be the shock of discovering that her children no longer want to bring friends home, because they are afraid of finding their mother drunk and ashamed of having anyone see her that way.

Once an alcoholic has made the decision to try to conquer his condition, there is still a long, hard road ahead. Our society holds so many temptations! At a party, others are drinking and enjoying themselves. Well-meaning friends may offer a hospitable drink. Scenes in movies and television plays show people drinking and remind the sober alcoholic of what he is missing. Often, alcohol has for many years been a way of coping with problems, of forgetting about worries and easing tensions. As the alcohol dependence grew, drinking itself created further problems. But once an alcoholic stops drinking, these problems do not all vanish automatically. They must be faced and worked through. An alcoholic may relapse, go on a drinking binge, and then have to start over again in his efforts to abstain.

An alcoholic who has decided to stop drinking may know that eventually he will feel more vital and healthy than he has for a long time. But at first he feels terrible. Alcohol abuse may have damaged his liver and left him easy prey to tuberculosis and other infectious diseases. Pellagra and other vitamin deficiency diseases may have developed, and curing them takes time. A subtler problem that has only recently been recognized is the disturbance of an alcoholic's sleep patterns. Prolonged abuse of alcohol, such as on a typical drinking bout, decreases the amount of dreaming sleep. Sleep researchers refer to this phase of sleep as REM sleep, because it is characterized by rapid eye movements. After alcohol is withdrawn, the amount of REM sleep increases; perhaps this "REM rebound," in extreme form, may be a factor in the hallucinations experienced during acute withdrawal symptoms. But the alcoholic recovering from a drinking binge also suffers from a lack of the deep phase of sleep. He sleeps fitfully, arousing readily and often. Studies of normal volunteers deprived of the deep phase of sleep have shown that they become restless and irritable. These effects may be observed in recovering alcoholics, and their insomnia and sleep disturbances may persist for as long as six months. Undoubtedly this is another factor contributing to the sudden cravings for a drink that periodically sweep over them.

To a growing degree, industry is providing motivation and help for alcoholics to seek treatment. It used to be customary in many businesses and industries to automatically fire employees whose drinking made them inefficient and dangerous workers. But employers are finding more and more that it is far more profitable to rehabilitate alcoholics than to train other people to take their place. In some companies, workers suspected of having a drinking problem are called in to talk with their supervisor. It has been found that it is most effective for the supervisor not to bring up the subject of problem drinking. Many alcoholics are defensive about their drinking. They will not admit, to themselves or others, that they are drinking destructively, and they make up elaborate alibis for absences from work or drops in production. (Typically an alcoholic's spouse will call up to say he or she has a mysterious "virus" when the real problem is a Monday hangover.) Instead, the supervisor will focus on the worker's absenteeism, poor sales record, or other work deficiencies that have begun to show up. Every opportunity is given to the worker to bring up the subject of alcohol. Finally, if necessary, the employee is told that he or she must either "shape up" or be suspended or fired. Job security seems to be one of the strongest motivations for an alcoholic. As soon as the worker admits to a drinking problem, he or she is referred to a rehabilitation program. At one time, ex-alcoholics found it hard to regain the respect of others. Fortunately, that attitude is now being replaced by admiration for someone who has licked the problem of alcoholism. The example of fellow workers who have "made it" is encouraging many alcoholics to seek help earlier.

Various approaches have been used to help alcoholics. Tranquilizers and other drugs may be useful in some cases, but care must be taken to avoid simply substituting one addiction for another. Psychotherapy, probing at the causes of alcoholism and attempting to work out alternative methods of coping with problems, has been used. Techniques of group psychotherapy, in which patients help one another to recover, are often effective, and they seem to work best when all the members of the group are alcoholics, rather than suffering from a variety of psychological problems.

Recently a school of thought called behavior modification therapy has developed in psychiatry, claiming that it is often too inefficient and time-consuming to try to delve into the long-buried causes of mental illness. Instead, an attempt is made to reeducate the person's aberrant behavior, permitting him to function effectively again. The techniques of behavior therapy are having some success in alcoholism. A typical approach is aversion therapy, the formation of negative associations with the behavior that is to be eliminated—in this case, drinking alcoholic beverages. The alcoholic may be given an injection of a drug that produces violent nausea after a few minutes. Then, with the appropriate timing, he is given a drink of alcohol. He drinks, and the nausea hits. After a number of repetitions of the experience, his mind associates drinking with unpleasant reactions, and he is less likely to take a drink. Mild but unpleasant electric shocks may be used in a similar way.

It has been found that patients' reactions in a hospital setting may be quite different from their reactions in a normal home or social environment. Therefore, aversion therapy is often conducted in a room specially decorated to simulate a bar or other typical drinking environment; the drinks are served by a bartender in standard drinking glasses, and various other props and background music may be used to reproduce as well as possible the conditions the alcoholics will encounter when they leave the hospital and try to "make it" on their own.

Another approach that has proved effective for some alcoholics is the use of a drug called Antabuse, or disulfiram. Under normal conditions, this drug does not produce any particular effect. But a person who drinks alcohol within a few days after taking Antabuse has an immediate reaction. His blood pressure first rises, then plunges. He flushes, feels faint, and is seized by a violent nausea. In especially severe reactions, he may collapse. Antabuse is a potentially dangerous drug, and must be used under a doctor's supervision. It does not prevent an alcoholic from drinking, but he knows that if he does, the results will be extremely unpleasant. He must make a conscious, positive decision to take the drug each time. But at least the major decision need be made only once every few days, rather than many times a day when the cravings hit.

One of the most effective approaches for coping with alcoholism is the organization called Alcoholics Anonymous (A.A.). It was started back in 1935, by alcoholics themselves, as a sort of mutual help group. Today it is estimated that there are more than 750,000 members of A.A. Alcoholics Anonymous charges no fees or membership dues. Members get together in local groups once or twice a week to discuss their past experiences and suggest ways to help one another. Some meetings are "closed" meetings, attended only by alcoholics or former alcoholics; other meetings are open to family and friends of alcoholics, who are encouraged to learn as much as possible about the disease and how the alcoholic can be helped. Mutual help is a keynote of A.A. The alcoholic is encouraged to call another member if he or she is having great difficulty overcoming an urge to drink; the A.A. member will help to talk it out and may even come over to sit with the alcoholic until the danger has passed.

It is a basic philosophy of Alcoholics Anonymous that alcoholism is a progressive disease, involving physical, mental, and spiritual aspects, and it can be arrested, although it cannot be cured. It is believed that an irreversible reaction has occurred in the alcoholic's body and that drinking alcohol sets up a craving for more alcohol. The alcoholic is urged to subject himself to a searching inner examination, to admit that he has wronged others and that his own life has become unmanageable, and to place himself in the power of some higher Being. It is recognized that the decision to renounce alcohol for life may be too terrifying for the alcoholic to make. Instead, the emphasis is placed on abstaining from drinking for twenty-four hours at a time. When a powerful urge to take a drink arises, the alcoholic need not resist or yield, but just put off the decision until "tomorrow."

Members of an alcoholic's family may be helped to gain understanding and aided in the day-to-day problems of coping by Al-Anon Family Groups, which are operated in association with A.A. Alateen groups are specially designed for teenagers who have alcoholic parents. All those who live with and love an alcoholic can find strength and comfort in the Al-Anon Serenity Prayer:

God grant me the serenity to accept the things I cannot change, the courage to change the things I can, and the wisdom to know the difference.

Recently some researchers have begun to challenge the basic premise of A.A. and many other specialists in alcoholism: that an alcoholic must never take another drink—that a single drink will doom the alcoholic to a repetition of the old pattern of alcohol abuse. A growing number of studies are focusing on efforts to transform alcoholics into social drinkers, rather than abstainers.

In one approach, aversion therapy is used not to link all drinking with negative feelings but instead to educate the alcoholic away from inappropriate and destructive drinking habits. In a cocktail lounge setting, the alcoholic is permitted to order as many drinks as he wants, of whatever kind. He receives an electric shock if he lapses into his old, alcohol-abusing habits—gulping a drink, for example, or ordering another drink too soon after finishing the last one. As the program progresses, the alcoholic may gradually be retrained in his drinking behavior, to order more dilute alcoholic beverages (a highball rather than a straight whiskey, for example), and to gain more sophistication about different kinds of alcoholic beverages, rather than drinking just one type of drink. Supportive counseling, teaching the alcoholic about other, less destructive ways of relieving tensions, helps to reinforce the shock sessions.

In a chemical approach to the problem of alcoholism, a research team at Rockland State Hospital in Orangeburg, New York, headed by Dr. Nathan S. Kline, has found that lithium treatments seem to prevent recurrent disabling drinking bouts. Before lithium was tried on alcoholics, it was found to be effective for patients with a mental condition called manic depressive disease. Often such patients alternate between periods of great elation and deep depression which have no apparent objective cause. Lithium is nontoxic enough to be given regularly over long periods of time, and when it is, it seems to smooth out the moods of manic depressive patients, permitting them to live normally. Since many alcoholics are depressed, it was decided to try lithium on them also. In the tests at Rockland State Hospital, two groups of alcoholic patients were given pills regularly. Some received lithium, while others received pills of an inactive substance—what scientists call a placebo. Neither the doctors nor the patients knew who was really receiving the lithium until afterward, when the results of the experiment were tallied. During the first year of the study, the alcoholics receiving lithium had only one-fourth as many disabling drinking bouts as those receiving the placebos, although they still continued to drink moderately. In the second year, only two patients receiving lithium had any disabling drinking bouts at all.

Many specialists in alcoholism view the idea that alcoholics can be converted to social drinkers with great skepticism. The long-term results of such approaches have yet to come in, and such treatments are not suitable for all alcoholics. (It may be significant that the Rockland State Hospital study started out with a group of seventy-three patients and ended with only twenty-one; more than two-thirds dropped out.) But there is hope that, at least sometime in the future, the question of "to drink or not to drink" will be a voluntary decision for former alcoholics as well.

Living with an Alcoholic Parent

The teen years can be a difficult time for anyone. Dramatic changes are occurring in the teenager's body and must be gradually adjusted to, while at the same time he is learning more about the world around him. More and more he is beginning to think for himself and learning to make his own decisions. He is beginning to try out adult roles, but he does not yet have the full rights and responsibilities of an adult. Understanding parents can do much to ease the transition from child to adult. But the teenager's adjustments are all the harder if one or both of his parents are alcoholics.

Alcoholism is an individual disease, but it does not affect just the alcoholic. Extra burdens, both emotional and financial, are thrown upon the members of an alcoholic's family, especially his or her spouse. The strain of coping may make the nonalcoholic parent tense and short-tempered. The intense involvement in trying to help the alcoholic may leave little time and energy to devote to the children in the family.

The older children in an alcoholic's family often become "substitute parents" for their younger brothers and sisters, dressing and feeding them and putting them to bed. They may take over many of the chores of the household and may help to care for the alcoholic parent. But a teenager should not try to take over completely for an alcoholic parent. The realization that he or she is needed may be the push that will help the parent seek aid in bringing his or her drinking under control.

In spite of all he or she tries to do, the child of an alcoholic may be made to feel unloved and unappreciated. There is a constant strain of uncertainty. The alcoholic parent may fly into sudden, unpredictable rages, while at other times he or she may try to make it up to the children by buying them expensive presents or making fanciful, unrealistic plans and promises. Problem drinking may jeopardize the alcoholic's job and add financial uncertainty to the family's burdens.

Problems of social adjustment are magnified for the children of an alcoholic. They may be afraid or ashamed to bring friends home, and may be inclined to turn down friends' invitations because they know they will not be able to invite their friends in turn. The nonalcoholic parent may be so used to worrying that he or she will worry unreasonably about teenagers in the family, too, and may demand minute-by-minute accounts of whom they see and where they go.

One special worry that children of alcoholics may have is, "Will I become an alcoholic too?" Some studies indicate that children of alcoholics have a higher risk of becoming alcoholics than children whose parents are not alcoholics; still, even the children of alcoholics are three or four times more likely *not* to have drinking problems than they are to have them. Scientists are not yet sure exactly what role heredity may play in alcoholism, but they do know that—as with many other diseases—it is not alcoholism itself that is inherited. If anything, it is a susceptibility to alcoholism that is inherited. But a person who knows he or she is susceptible to something can be on guard against it.

Problems always seem more difficult to bear when we feel that no one else is suffering from any problems like ours. Confiding in a close friend can help a teenager to cope with an alcoholic parent. The troubled teenager may be amazed to find that people whose parents are not alcoholic also have problems, some of them very similar to his own. Counselors at school may provide a sympathetic ear and may arrange for help from community-sponsored family services. Alateen meetings bring teenagers with alcoholic parents together with others who share their problems. Such meetings are often scheduled on the same nights and in the same building as Alcoholics Anonymous meetings. Parents attending the A.A. meetings provide transportation for their children, and both parents and teenagers have the feeling of working together to bring their problems under control.

A Personal Decision

It is estimated that one out of every fifteen young people will eventually become an alcoholic. What are your chances of winding up on the wrong end of those statistics?

The majority of adults in our culture do drink, and most of them will never become problem drinkers. Yet so far, no one is able to tell beforehand which one out of fifteen is in danger.

One sure way to avoid becoming an alcoholic is never to drink at all. But many people feel that such a decision means missing out on one of the pleasures of life. On the basis of the evidence available so far, drinking in moderation seems to be a reasonably harmless pleasure. To drink or not to drink should be a personal decision. You should not allow others to pressure you into a decision, either way, but you should decide knowing the facts about alcohol.

If your decision is to drink, there are some

important things to consider. Drinking, like other privileges of adult life, carries with it certain responsibilities. You should not drink in such a way that you may cause harm to others. Driving a car after drinking excessively is not responsible behavior. (And for a teenager, even a "couple of beers" may be enough to impair driving ability to a dangerous degree.) If you want to drink at a social affair, arrange beforehand for some alternate means of transportation. A decision to drive made under the influence of alcohol is often an unwise one, since euphoria may make you convinced that you can do anything. It might be wise to limit your drinking and do your drinking early: the alcohol in each standard drink of distilled spirits or bottle of beer takes about two hours to be completely eliminated from the body.

Avoiding drunkenness is another aspect of responsible drinking behavior. Without the controls of your higher brain, you might say or do things you would regret afterward.

Be familiar with the warning signs of problem drinking. Alcoholism usually develops over a period of years. If you find that you are drinking more and more often, if you are drinking mainly to forget your troubles, or just for the sake of drinking—it is time to call a halt and analyze just where you are heading. You may be the one in fifteen who cannot handle alcohol. Remember that alcoholics do not harm only themselves. They have the potential for hurting their families and friends, fellow workers, and innocent bystanders on the streets and highways.

Drinking should be a personal decision—make yours a wise one!

For Further Information

If you need help on a personal or family problem of alcoholism, you will probably be able to find a listing of an Alcoholics Anonymous (A.A.) group in your local telephone book. If not, you can write to:

> Alcoholics Anonymous
> General Service Office
> Box 459
> Grand Central Station
> New York, N. Y. 10017

Further information about various aspects of alcohol problems may be found in the following books:

Al-Anon Faces Alcoholism, New York, Al-Anon, 1973.
Alcohol and Health (First Special Report to the U.S. Congress from the Secretary of Health, Education, and Welfare), Washington, D.C., DHEW, 1971.
Alcohol and Health: New Knowledge (Second Special

Report to the U.S. Congress from the Secretary of Health, Education, and Welfare), Washington, D.C., DHEW, 1974.

Ayars, Albert L. and Milgram, Gail G., *The Teenager and Alcohol*, New York, Richards Rosen Press, 1970.

Bacon, Margaret and Jones, Mary Brush, *Teen-Age Drinking*, New York, Thomas Y. Crowell, 1968.

Block, Marvin, A., M.D., *Alcohol and Alcoholism: Drinking and Dependence*, Belmont, Calif., Wadsworth, 1970.

Brecher, Edward M., and the Editors of *Consumer Reports, Licit and Illicit Drugs*, Orangeburg, N. Y., Consumers Union, 1972.

Cahalan, Don, *Problem Drinkers*, San Francisco, Calif., Josey Bass, 1970.

Carroll, Charles R., *Alcohol: Use, Non-Use, and Abuse*, Dubuque, Iowa, William C. Brown, 1970.

Chafetz, Morris E., Blane, Howard T., and Hill, Marjorie J., *Frontiers of Alcoholism*, New York, Science House, 1970.

Fort, Joel, *Alcohol: Our Biggest Drug Problem*, New York, McGraw-Hill, 1973.

Hornik, Edith Lynn, *You and Your Alcoholic Parent*, New York, Association Press, 1974.

Hyde, Margaret O., *Alcohol: Drink or Drug?* New York, McGraw-Hill, 1974.

Plaut, Thomas F. A., and the Cooperative Commission on the Study of Alcoholism, *Alcohol Problems: A Report to*

the Nation, New York, Oxford University Press, 1967.
Roueche, Berton, *Alcohol: The Neutral Spirit*, Boston, Little Brown, 1960; Berkeley Medallion Edition, 1971.
Whitney, Elizabeth D., *The Lonely Sickness*, Boston, Beacon Press, 1965.

Index

A.A. *See* Alcoholics Anonymous
absorption of alcohol, 30–32; from intestines, 30, 31; from stomach, 30
accidents, drinking and, 46, 70, 72–76
acetaldehyde, 39, 40
acetic acid, 39
addiction to alcohol, 85
Ahtee, Liise, 98
Al-Anon Family Groups, 109
Al-Anon Serenity Prayer, 109
Alateen groups, 109, 116
alcohol: attitudes toward, 11–12, 64–68; calorie content of, 39; chemical formula of, 15; elimination of, 38, 40; food value of, 39–40; history of, 50–58; origin of word, 52; oxidation of, 39; taste of, 62. *See also* effects of alcohol
alcohol abuse: effects on body of, 46–49; patterns of, 92
alcohol content: of beer, 19, 26; of cocktail, 26; of distilled spirits, 17, 19, 23–24, 28–29; of fermented beverages, 17; of whiskey, 19, 26; of wine, 19, 21, 26
alcohol dependence, 68
alcohol poisoning, 38
alcoholic parent, 113–116
alcoholics: characteristics of, 84–85, 86–88; ratio of male to female, 59–60; treatment of, 101–112
Alcoholics Anonymous (A.A.), 87, 90, 108–110, 116, 121

alcoholism, 83–100; causes of, 93–94; development of, 86, 88–92; as a disease, 94–95; as a health problem, 12; stages of, 88–92; tests for, 86–88; treatment for, 101–112
alcohols, types of, 16
aldehydes, 74–75
ale, 17, 19–20
American Medical Association, 94
amphetamines, 12, 45
Antabuse (disulfiram), 107
antidiuretic hormone (ADH), 37
antihistamines, 44
Anti-Saloon League, 55
attitudes toward drinking: Americans', 68; ethnic groups', 64–68; industry's, 104–105; religious groups', 60–61
automation, drinking and, 68
aversion therapy, 106, 110
Aztecs, 52

B vitamins, 96
Bacchus, 51
barbiturates, 12, 44
bathtub gin, 58
beer, 17, 26, 29, 31, 54, 59, 78; alcohol content of, 26; making of, 19–20
behavior modification therapy, 106
Bible, alcohol in, 51–52
birth defects, 48
blackouts, 49, 88, 89
blood alcohol level, 29, 37, 70, 71, 72, 73, 74, 76; of drivers, 74

INDEX

reflexes, 35
religion, drinking and, 60–61
religious rituals, drinking in, 61, 65
REM rebound, alcohol withdrawal and, 104
remedies for drunkenness, 40–41
research on alcoholism, 95–100; animal, 97–100
"revolving door" policy, 101
RNA, 49
Roaring Twenties, 58
rum, 25, 53
rye, 24

sake, 17
Scotch whisky, 24
serotonin, 99
sexes, drinking practices of, 59–60, 78
sexual activity, 36, 81
Shakespeare, William, 36
sherry, 21
Skid Row, 83, 84
sleep disturbances, alcohol withdrawal and, 104
slivovitz, 25
smoking, drinking and, 45–46
sobering up, 40–41
social drinking, 59–68; reasons for, 63
sodium acetate, 41
sparkling wines, 22–23
spirits, 23
spree drinker, 92–93
starch, 19
steady drinker, 92–93
stimulants, 44–45
Stokes, Peter, 47
stomach, 30
stout, 20
sugar, 15, 19, 21

sweet wines, 21
synergistic effect, 44

tchoo, 17
teenage drinking, 13–14, 77–82; parents' attitudes toward, 79–80; practices, 78–79; reasons for, 63, 79–81
temperance movement, 55–57
Ten Nights in a Bar Room, 56
Tewari, Sujata, 48
tolerance to alcohol, 33
traffic accidents and drinking. See drinking and driving
tranquilizers: and alcohol, 44; in treatment of alcoholism, 106
tuberculosis, 103
tunnel vision, 71

urinary tract, 36
urination, 36–37

violence, drinking and, 36, 46, 63
vitamins: and alcohol abuse, 48; as remedy for drunkenness, 40–41
vodka, 24–25
Volstead Act, 57

"wets" and "drys," 57
whiskey, 19, 24, 26; alcohol content of, 26; blended, 24; straight, 24
"whiskey voice," 29
white blood cells, 48
wine, 17, 19, 21–23, 26, 31, 54, 59, 61, 78; alcohol content of, 21, 26; composition of, 21; making of, 22
withdrawal from alcohol, 41–42
Women's Christian Temperance Union, 55, 83

yeast, 15, 16

ALVIN SILVERSTEIN, born in New York City and raised in Brooklyn, developed an early interest in science. He received his B.A. from Brooklyn College, his M.A. from the University of Pennsylvania, and his Ph.D. from New York University. He is Professor of Biology at the Staten Island Community College of City University of New York.

VIRGINIA SILVERSTEIN grew up in Philadelphia and received her B.A. from the University of Pennsylvania. Since her marriage, she has worked as a free-lance translator of Russian scientific literature, doing extensive work for government and private agencies.

The Silversteins, who have collaborated on over thirty science books for young readers, live on a farm near Lebanon, New Jersey, with their six children.

DR. GAIL GLEASON MILGRAM is an Associate Professor at the Center of Alcohol Studies at Rutgers University where she has prepared an *Annotated Bibliography of Alcohol Education Material.* As Consultant to the New Jersey Department of Health's Alcohol Control Program, she coauthored a reference book, *Alcohol Education Resource Unit.* In addition she is the coauthor of *The Teenager and Alcohol* and the author of several articles on teenage drinking and alcohol education. In 1969, Dr. Milgram completed an extensive research project which gathered information on teenage drinking and alcohol education from school administrators, teachers, parents, and teenage students in a select community. One of the significant findings of this study was the view expressed by teenagers and adults that a need existed for an objective presentation for teenagers of the facts about alcohol.